BACK & FORTH

Pair Activities for Language Development

Adrian S. Palmer
University of Utah

Theodore S. Rodgers
University of Hawaii

Judy Winn-Bell Olsen
City College of San Francisco

Alta Book Center Publishers—San Francisco
14 Adrian Court, Burlingame, California 94010 USA

Editor: Helen Munch
Production: The Compage Company
Designer: Joy Dickinson
Illustrator: Zahid Sardar
Cover designer: Leigh McLellan

Printed in the United States of America

ISBN 1-882483-73-1

© 1999 by Alta Book Center Publishers—San Francisco
14 Adrian Court, Burlingame, California 94010
Phone: 1 800 ALTA/ESL or 650.692.1285
Fax: 1 800 ALTA/FAX or 650.692.4654
Web: www.altaesl.com
Email Address: info@altaesl.com

Acknowledgments

The authors would like to thank the following people for their participation in this project: The members of the Department of Foreign Languages of Khon Kaen University, Thailand, for their help in producing and testing the original version of the materials; George Trosper, for his editorial help in reorganizing and rewriting; and Philip Raue in Singapore, Claudio Souza in Brazil, Suzanne Griffin in Seattle, Washington, USA, Mary Ann Christison in Salt Lake City, Utah, USA and Dennis Johnson and Yvonne Safwat in San Francisco, California USA for their helpful comments during the field testing of these materials.

Contents

Continued

Introduction

ABOUT THIS BOOK

Back & Forth contains 32 reproducible exercises designed to help intermediate ESL students improve their listening and speaking skills. The exercises are short, interactive, and highly focused, requiring students to communicate with one another to complete a specific task. Students work with partners in pairs (or in paired groups*), each partner having slightly different information from that possessed by the other. The information appears on separate exercise pages, one for Partner A and one for Partner B. In each exercise, accurate listening is as important as speaking in the completion of the task.

The Student

The "intermediate" student for whom this book is written includes adult non-university and secondary school students, age 14 years and above, as well as advanced beginners in university intensive English programs. Students should have some experience in communicative language use, or a desire to develop it, an active vocabulary of at least 500 words, and the ability to relate the spoken to the written word in English. *Back & Forth* will be most useful in classes where the emphasis is on developing confidence and interaction skills, and in conversation, listening, pronunciation, and oral grammar practice classes.

The Activities and Exercises

The pair activities in *Back & Forth* are divided into four types or Parts. Each Part features eight reproducible exercises.

In Part One, "Pronunciation and Aural Discrimination," students produce and discriminate between single vowels, consonants, and consonant clusters in various positions.

In Part Two, "Describing a Picture," students match a picture to its description, and in Part Three, "Asking and Answering Questions About a Picture," students formulate questions and answers about a picture. The pictures are of four types, each requiring a different student response:

1. Pictures of objects (clocks, tables) and articles of clothing (shirts, hats) require students to describe physical features and characteristics.

2. Pictures of animals or of two individuals interacting require students to express semantic relationships involving location, agent, instrument, subject, object, possession, and so forth.

---

*In paired groups, two or three students collaborate on producing whatever is required for Partner A or Partner B. This approach is particularly useful in classes where there are both strong and weak students or where newcomers enter after the class is already familiar with the text.

3. Pictures of abstract forms and geometrical shapes require students to describe spatial relationships.

4. Pictures suggesting linguistic puzzles require students to use adjective clauses or other modification structures.

Each exercise includes six sets of four pictures each and a combination of the four picture types.

In Part Four, "Constructing Meaningful Dialogs," students select appropriate questions or statements in order to construct dialogs that make sense. The exercises deal with such everyday topics as the weather, illnesses, appointments, and so forth.

Introducing each Part is a reproducible Sample Exercise to be done with the entire class. (Part One also includes reproducible Word Lists for each student.) Following each Sample Exercise are eight different reproducible exercises that allow for extensive practice of each activity. Each exercise consists of two pages, one for Partner A and one for Partner B.

The performance of the exercises is consistent from Part to Part. One partner performs the activity—pronouncing words, describing a picture, asking questions about a picture, or beginning a dialog— while the other partner listens. The second partner then responds by marking an answer on his or her exercise page or by answering a question or statement. The partners alternately perform the activity until it ends, at which point they compare answers. They then repeat the exercise with a new partner or with the same partner using different items or different exercise pages.

The exercises are intended for repeated use by different student pairs or paired groups throughout the school term. There is no particular order of difficulty or of presentation of the exercise material within the text, though the exercises themselves are deliberately controlled.

HOW TO USE THIS BOOK

The first time through any activity may be a little rough. If pair activities are new to you and your students, here are some suggestions to help you manage the first few classes.

Before Class

- Select an activity (for example, describing a picture) and read the instructions. Note that the language is directed to the student. You may wish to simplify or to paraphrase the language when you present the activity to your students.

- Be sure to read the notes To the Teacher at the beginning of each part for additional information about each activity (see pp. 8, 36, 56, and 77).

- Duplicate enough copies of the Sample Exercise for your class and, if possible, make a transparency for use with an overhead projector. (Most copy machines make transparencies the same way they make paper copies. If you are unfamiliar with the process, check with the company that services your school's copy machines.)
- Duplicate enough copies of one exercise—for Partners A and B—to distribute in class. (In Part One, you will need copies of the Word Lists as well; all students receive the same Word List.) You might also want to make additional copies so that each student can take home both the Partner A and Partner B pages to study and to practice after class.

During Class

- If you prepared a transparency of the Sample Exercise, project it on the wall or blackboard. Otherwise, make a large drawing of the Sample Exercise on the board.

- Divide the class into Partners A and B and lead students through the examples in the Sample Exercise.

- Distribute the Sample Exercise. Once students have understood the examples, hand out the first duplicated exercise, one page each for Partners A and B.

- Don't be alarmed if, at first, some students seem bewildered or unsure of themselves and want to look at each other's pages.

- Encourage questions and discussion about the activity and procedure. Such discussion is part of the expected interaction; questions will help you judge individual student progress.

- Enforce the rules: no looking at each other's page while an exercise is in progress; no speaking of languages other than English, and so forth.

- Once students have finished an exercise, have them change partners and repeat the exercise. The change of partners is important because everyone in class will communicate a bit differently. Students need to become familiar with a variety of communication styles. The change will also enable quicker learners to help slower learners perform the activity.

The Next Class

- Repeat the activity using another exercise. Gradually, through practice, students will become more comfortable with each activity.

- Introduce another exercise and, later, introduce a new activity type. Reintroduce the activities and exercises throughout the school term, reviewing instructions and vocabulary as needed.

YOUR ATTITUDE AND APPROACH

The activities in *Back & Forth* are meant to be fun for your students. You can help establish a pleasant and positive classroom atmosphere by your own attitude and approach. Experiment to find out which activity arouses the most enthusiasm. Do students prefer working one-on-one in pairs, or in paired groups with several students collaborating? Do they prefer being timed or completing the exercises at their own pace? Are student scores made public or kept private for the individual student? By trying to adjust to the learning styles of your students, you can make the activities more useful and enjoyable for the entire class.

The four types of activities provide at least two very different kinds of opportunities for language practice and language acquisition from meaningful contexts. One kind occurs within the activity itself, as suggested by its title; the other occurs outside of the activity, as a sort of by-product. This second opportunity for language practice and acquisition develops as students comment on the activity, prepare to perform it, have difficulty doing it, try to explain it to somebody else, or discuss it with their partners. This kind of language or communication may occur between students and teacher or among the students themselves. In either case, *any* kind of communication about the activities or exercises is to be encouraged. The more discussion that occurs, the more general English communication skills will develop, and the more successful student performance of the activities will be. Student-initiated talk about the activities is considered as valuable as actual performance itself.

PART ONE
PRONUNCIATION AND AURAL DISCRIMINATION

To the Teacher

1. Since the focus of Part One is Pronunciation and Aural Discrimination, you are not expected to spend much class time explaining vocabulary. As the instructions to the students state, "Do not worry about the meaning of the words right now." Stress the correct pronunciation of the underlined words and emphasize that certain sounds will be more difficult for some students than for others, depending on the students' native languages.

2. When you introduce this activity, be sure to give each student a copy of the Word List as well as the Sample Exercise page.

3. Remind students not to look at each other's pages until the exercise is over.

Sample Exercise 1

The exercises in Part One will give you practice in speaking clearly and in listening carefully.

WHAT TO DO

You and your partner will each receive an exercise page. On each page there will be underlined words for you to pronounce and choices for you to make. Look at example 1, below.

1. **If you are Partner A, pronounce:**

   ball
   <u>bit</u>
   bat

   If you are Partner B, listen and mark:

   bat (   )
   ball (   )
   bit (   )

The correct choice is "bit." Partner B should mark the answer (X) in the space provided. Now try example 2. This time Partner A listens.

2. **If you are Partner A, listen and mark:**

   flute (   )
   fruit (   )
   food (   )

   If you are Partner B, pronounce:

   fruit
   <u>food</u>
   flute

The correct choice is "food." Partner A should mark the answer (X) in the space provided. Now try examples 3 and 4. This time *you* select the words to pronounce. Remember to speak clearly and to repeat the words until your partner understands what you are saying.

3. **If you are Partner A, pronounce:**

   same
   save
   safe

   If you are Partner B, listen and mark:

   save (   )
   safe (   )
   same (   )

4. **If you are Partner A, listen and mark:**

   lesser (   )
   lever (   )
   letter (   )

   If you are Partner B, pronounce:

   letter
   lesser
   lever

When you finish an exercise, review your answers with your partner. Be sure to discuss your mistakes and any problems you had. Then, repeat the exercise with the same partner (exchange papers) or with a different partner, and choose different words to pronounce. Mark your answers with a new mark (✔).

Word List 1.1

Instructions: The following words contain sounds that are difficult for many non-native English speakers to pronounce. Repeat each word after your teacher. Listen carefully to how it is pronounced. Do not worry about the meaning of the words right now. You can look them up in your dictionary later, if you like.

1. cent
   sends
   sense

2. saver
   safer
   saber

3. tea
   tree
   three

4. hat
   hot
   hut

5. put
   puss
   push

6. matter
   madder
   manner

7. chew
   shoe
   zoo

8. eat
   it
   ate

9. math
   match
   mat

10. rower
    roller
    roar

11. clop
    crop
    cop

12. nog
    knock
    knocks

13. cheap
    jeep
    sheep

14. meat
    mitt
    met

15. figs
    fix
    fits

16. cooed
    could
    code

Exercise 1.1

Instructions: Pronounce the underlined words for your partner, and listen as your partner pronounces other words for you. If necessary, ask your partner to repeat. Mark an "X" next to the word you hear. Do not look at your partner's page while you are doing this exercise!

1. **Listen and mark:**
   cent (   )
   sends (   )
   sense (   )

2. **Pronounce:**
   saber
   saver
   safer

3. **Listen and mark:**
   tea   (   )
   tree (   )
   three (   )

4. **Pronounce:**
   hut
   hot
   hat

5. **Listen and mark:**
   put   (   )
   puss (   )
   push (   )

6. **Pronounce**
   madder
   manner
   matter

7. **Listen and mark:**
   chew (   )
   shoe (   )
   zoo   (   )

8. **Pronounce:**
   it
   eat
   ate

9. **Listen and mark:**
   math (   )
   match (   )
   mat   (   )

10. **Pronounce:**
    roar
    roller
    rower

11. **Listen and mark:**
    clop (   )
    crop (   )
    cop   (   )

12. **Pronounce:**
    nog
    knocks
    knock

13. **Listen and mark:**
    cheap (   )
    jeep (   )
    sheep (   )

14. **Pronounce:**
    meat
    met
    mitt

15. **Listen and mark:**
    figs (   )
    fix   (   )
    fits (   )

16. **Pronounce:**
    code
    cooed
    could

When you finish this exercise, show your page to your partner and compare your answers. Are they the same? Which ones did you miss? Practice pronouncing the words. If you are not sure of the pronunciation, ask your teacher for help. If there is time, do the exercise again, but choose different words to pronounce and make different marks on your page.

Exercise 1.1

Instructions: Pronounce the under-lined words for your partner, and listen as your partner pronounces other words for you. If necessary, ask your partner to repeat. Mark an "X" next to the word you hear. Do not look at your partner's page while you are doing this exercise!

1. **Pronounce:**
   sends
   sense
   cent

2. **Listen and mark:**
   saver ( )
   safer ( )
   saber ( )

3. **Pronounce:**
   tree
   three
   tea

4. **Listen and mark:**
   hat ( )
   hot ( )
   hut ( )

5. **Pronounce:**
   puss
   put
   push

6. **Listen and mark:**
   matter ( )
   madder ( )
   manner ( )

7. **Pronounce:**
   chew
   zoo
   shoe

8. **Listen and mark:**
   eat ( )
   it ( )
   ate ( )

9. **Pronounce:**
   mat
   match
   math

10. **Listen and mark:**
    rower ( )
    roller ( )
    roar ( )

11. **Pronounce:**
    cop
    clop
    crop

12. **Listen and mark:**
    nog ( )
    knock ( )
    knocks ( )

13. **Pronounce:**
    sheep
    jeep
    cheap

14. **Listen and mark:**
    meat ( )
    mitt ( )
    met ( )

15. **Pronounce:**
    figs
    fits
    fix

16. **Listen and mark:**
    cooed ( )
    could ( )
    code ( )

When you finish this exercise, show your page to your partner and com-pare your answers. Are they the same? Which ones did you miss? Practice pronouncing the words. If you are not sure of the pronuncia-tion, ask your teacher for help. If there is time, do the exercise again, but choose different words to pro-nounce and make different marks on your page.

Word List 1.2

Instructions: The following words contain sounds that are difficult for many non-native English speakers to pronounce. Repeat each word after your teacher. Listen carefully to how it is pronounced. Do not worry about the meaning of the words right now. You can look them up in your dictionary later, if you like.

1. ways
   wise
   was

2. dipper
   dimmer
   dinner

3. came
   cape
   cave

4. same
   Sam
   psalm

5. sink
   zinc
   think

6. collect
   correct
   connect

7. Lou
   loop
   loon

8. rat
   rot
   rut

9. joke
   choke
   yoke

10. bags
    bans
    bangs

11. waste
    wage
    wake

12. beat
    bit
    bet

13. lock
    rock
    dock

14. tempted
    tented
    tended

15. rub
    rough
    rum

16. hoe
    foe
    woe

Exercise 1.2

Instructions: Pronounce the underlined words for your partner, and listen as your partner pronounces other words for you. If necessary, ask your partner to repeat. Mark an "X" next to the word you hear. Do not look at your partner's page while you are doing this exercise!

1. Pronounce:
was
wise
ways

2. Listen and mark:
dipper ( )
dimmer ( )
dinner ( )

3. Pronounce:
cape
cave
came

4. Listen and mark:
same ( )
Sam ( )
psalm ( )

5. Pronounce:
zinc
think
sink

6. Listen and mark:
collect ( )
correct ( )
connect ( )

7. Pronounce:
loon
loop
Lou

8. Listen and mark:
rat ( )
rot ( )
rut ( )

9. Pronounce:
choke
yoke
joke

10. Listen and mark:
bags ( )
bans ( )
bangs ( )

11. Pronounce:
wake
wage
waste

12. Listen and mark:
beat ( )
bit ( )
bet ( )

13. Pronounce:
dock
rock
lock

14. Listen and mark:
tempted ( )
tented ( )
tended ( )

15. Pronounce:
rub
rum
rough

16. Listen and mark:
hoe ( )
foe ( )
woe ( )

When you finish this exercise, show your page to your partner and compare your answers. Are they the same? Which ones did you miss? Practice pronouncing the words. If you are not sure of the pronunciation, ask your teacher for help. If there is time, do the exercise again, but choose different words to pronounce and make different marks on your page.

Exercise 1.2

Instructions: Pronounce the under-lined words for your partner, and listen as your partner pronounces other words for you. If necessary, ask your partner to repeat. Mark an "X" next to the word you hear. Do not look at your partner's page while you are doing this exercise!

1. **Listen and mark:**
   ways ( )
   wise ( )
   was ( )

2. **Pronounce:**
   dimmer
   dipper
   dinner

3. **Listen and mark:**
   came ( )
   cape ( )
   cave ( )

4. **Pronounce:**
   Sam
   psalm
   same

5. **Listen and mark:**
   sink ( )
   zinc ( )
   think ( )

6. **Pronounce:**
   connect
   collect
   correct

7. **Listen and mark:**
   Lou ( )
   loop ( )
   loon ( )

8. **Pronounce:**
   rut
   rot
   rat

9. **Listen and mark:**
   joke ( )
   choke ( )
   yoke ( )

10. **Pronounce:**
    bangs
    bags
    bans

11. **Listen and mark:**
    waste ( )
    wage ( )
    wake ( )

12. **Pronounce:**
    bet
    bit
    beat

13. **Listen and mark:**
    lock ( )
    rock ( )
    dock ( )

14. **Pronounce:**
    tented
    tempted
    tended

15. **Listen and mark:**
    rub ( )
    rough ( )
    rum ( )

16. **Pronounce:**
    foe
    woe
    hoe

When you finish this exercise, show your page to your partner and com-pare your answers. Are they the same? Which ones did you miss? Practice pronouncing the words. If you are not sure of the pronuncia-tion, ask your teacher for help. If there is time, do the exercise again, but choose different words to pro-nounce and make different marks on your page.

Word List 1.3

Instructions: The following words contain sounds that are difficult for many non-native English speakers to pronounce. Repeat each word after your teacher. Listen carefully to how it is pronounced. Do not worry about the meaning of the words right now. You can look them up in your dictionary later, if you like.

1. sting
   string
   spring

2. hams
   hands
   hangs

3. base
   beige
   bathe

4. time
   Tom
   tame

5. band
   bland
   brand

6. nipple
   nibble
   nimble

7. deaf
   debt
   depth

8. boot
   boat
   bought

9. skiis
   squeeze
   sneeze

10. massing
    matching
    mashing

11. log
    logged
    locked

12. green
    grin
    grain

13. seal
    squeal
    zeal

14. click
    quick
    crick

15. need
    niece
    neat

16. streak
    strike
    stroke

Exercise 1.3

Instructions: Pronounce the underlined words for your partner, and listen as your partner pronounces other words for you. If necessary, ask your partner to repeat. Mark an "X" next to the word you hear. Do not look at your partner's page while you are doing this exercise!

1. Listen and mark:
sting ( )
string ( )
spring ( )

2. Pronounce:
hands
hangs
hams

3. Listen and mark:
base ( )
beige ( )
bathe ( )

4. Pronounce:
Tom
tame
time

5. Listen and mark:
band ( )
bland ( )
brand ( )

6. Pronounce:
nipple
nimble
nibble

7. Listen and mark:
deaf ( )
debt ( )
depth ( )

8. Pronounce:
boat
bought
boot

9. Listen and mark:
skiis ( )
squeeze ( )
sneeze ( )

10. Pronounce:
matching
mashing
massing

11. Listen and mark:
log ( )
logged ( )
locked ( )

12. Pronounce:
grain
grin
green

13. Listen and mark:
seal ( )
squeal ( )
zeal ( )

14. Pronounce:
crick
quick
click

15. Listen and mark:
need ( )
niece ( )
neat ( )

16. Pronounce:
stroke
strike
streak

When you finish this exercise, show your page to your partner and compare your answers. Are they the same? Which ones did you miss? Practice pronouncing the words. If you are not sure of the pronunciation, ask your teacher for help. If there is time, do the exercise again, but choose different words to pronounce and make different marks on your page.

Exercise 1.3
PARTNER **B**

Instructions: Pronounce the underlined words for your partner, and listen as your partner pronounces other words for you. If necessary, ask your partner to repeat. Mark an "X" next to the word you hear. Do not look at your partner's page while you are doing this exercise!

1. **Pronounce:**
   string
   spring
   sting

2. **Listen and mark:**
   hams ( )
   hands ( )
   hangs ( )

3. **Pronounce:**
   bathe
   beige
   base

4. **Listen and mark:**
   time ( )
   Tom ( )
   tame ( )

5. **Pronounce:**
   band
   brand
   bland

6. **Listen and mark:**
   nipple ( )
   nibble ( )
   nimble ( )

7. **Pronounce:**
   debt
   deaf
   depth

8. **Listen and mark:**
   boot ( )
   boat ( )
   bought ( )

9. **Pronounce:**
   sneeze
   squeeze
   skiis

10. **Listen and mark:**
    massing ( )
    matching ( )
    mashing ( )

11. **Pronounce:**
    logged
    locked
    log

12. **Listen and mark:**
    green ( )
    grin ( )
    grain ( )

13. **Pronounce:**
    seal
    zeal
    squeal

14. **Listen and mark:**
    click ( )
    quick ( )
    crick ( )

15. **Pronounce:**
    neat
    niece
    need

16. **Listen and mark:**
    streak ( )
    strike ( )
    stroke ( )

When you finish this exercise, show your page to your partner and compare your answers. Are they the same? Which ones did you miss? Practice pronouncing the words. If you are not sure of the pronunciation, ask your teacher for help. If there is time, do the exercise again, but choose different words to pronounce and make different marks on your page.

Word List 1.4

Instructions: The following words contain sounds that are difficult for many non-native English speakers to pronounce. Repeat each word after your teacher. Listen carefully to how it is pronounced. Do not worry about the meaning of the words right now. You can look them up in your dictionary later, if you like.

1. food
   flute
   fruit

2. raving
   railing
   raising

3. wings
   winged
   winked

4. bleed
   bled
   blood

5. vine
   fine
   wine

6. lazy
   lady
   lacy

7. rims
   ribs
   rips

8. wheat
   wit
   wet

9. go
   glow
   grow

10. winging
    winning
    willing

11. spool
    spook
    spoon

12. cream
    crime
    chrome

13. year
    jeer
    cheer

14. sinks
    sings
    sins

15. toot
    tote
    taught

16. aced
    aides
    A's

Exercise 1.4

Instructions: Pronounce the underlined words for your partner, and listen as your partner pronounces other words for you. If necessary, ask your partner to repeat. Mark an "X" next to the word you hear. Do not look at your partner's page while you are doing this exercise!

1. Pronounce:
food
fruit
flute

2. Listen and mark:
raving ( )
railing ( )
raising ( )

3. Pronounce:
winked
winged
wings

4. Listen and mark:
bleed ( )
bled ( )
blood ( )

5. Pronounce:
wine
vine
fine

6. Listen and mark:
lazy ( )
lady ( )
lacy ( )

7. Pronounce:
ribs
rims
rips

8. Listen and mark:
wheat ( )
wit ( )
wet ( )

9. Pronounce:
go
grow
glow

10. Listen and mark:
winging ( )
winning ( )
willing ( )

11. Pronounce:
spook
spool
spoon

12. Listen and mark:
cream ( )
crime ( )
chrome ( )

13. Pronounce:
jeer
cheer
year

14. Listen and mark:
sinks ( )
sings ( )
sins ( )

15. Pronounce:
taught
toot
tote

16. Listen and mark:
aced ( )
aides ( )
A's ( )

When you finish this exercise, show your page to your partner and compare your answers. Are they the same? Which ones did you miss? Practice pronouncing the words. If you are not sure of the pronunciation, ask your teacher for help. If there is time, do the exercise again, but choose different words to pronounce and make different marks on your page.

Exercise 1.4

Instructions: Pronounce the underlined words for your partner, and listen as your partner pronounces other words for you. If necessary, ask your partner to repeat. Mark an "X" next to the word you hear. Do not look at your partner's page while you are doing this exercise!

1. Listen and mark:
food ( )
flute ( )
fruit ( )

2. Pronounce:
raising
raving
railing

3. Listen and mark:
wings ( )
winged ( )
winked ( )

4. Pronounce:
blood
bled
bleed

5. Listen and mark:
vine ( )
fine ( )
wine ( )

6. Pronounce:
lacy
lazy
lady

7. Listen and mark:
rims ( )
ribs ( )
rips ( )

8. Pronounce:
wet
wheat
wit

9. Listen and mark:
go ( )
glow ( )
grow ( )

10. Pronounce:
willing
winning
winging

11. Listen and mark:
spool ( )
spook ( )
spoon ( )

12. Pronounce:
crime
chrome
cream

13. Listen and mark:
year ( )
jeer ( )
cheer ( )

14. Pronounce:
sins
sings
sinks

15. Listen and mark:
toot ( )
tote ( )
taught ( )

16. Pronounce:
A's
aced
aides

When you finish this exercise, show your page to your partner and compare your answers. Are they the same? Which ones did you miss? Practice pronouncing the words. If you are not sure of the pronunciation, ask your teacher for help. If there is time, do the exercise again, but choose different words to pronounce and make different marks on your page.

Word List 1.5

Instructions: The following words contain sounds that are difficult for many non-native English speakers to pronounce. Repeat each word after your teacher. Listen carefully to how it is pronounced. Do not worry about the meaning of the words right now. You can look them up in your dictionary later, if you like.

1. van
   fan
   ban

2. piggy
   picky
   pinky

3. lax
   lagged
   lacked

4. we
   why
   weigh

5. jewel
   dual
   yule

6. witty
   witchy
   wispy

7. clothe
   clothes
   closed

8. nut
   not
   note

9. thick
   tick
   Dick

10. basked
    bashed
    backed

11. mole
    more
    moan

12. found
    fond
    phoned

13. churl
    girl
    whirl

14. rougher
    rubber
    rudder

15. taps
    tapped
    tabs

16. ale
    owl
    oil

Exercise 1.5

Instructions: Pronounce the under-lined words for your partner, and listen as your partner pronounces other words for you. If necessary, ask your partner to repeat. Mark an "X" next to the word you hear. Do not look at your partner's page while you are doing this exercise!

1. **Listen and mark:**
   van ( )
   fan ( )
   ban ( )

2. **Pronounce:**
   pinky
   picky
   piggy

3. **Listen and mark:**
   lax ( )
   lagged ( )
   lacked ( )

4. **Pronounce:**
   why
   weigh
   we

5. **Listen and mark:**
   jewel ( )
   dual ( )
   yule ( )

6. **Pronounce:**
   witchy
   wispy
   witty

7. **Listen and mark:**
   clothe ( )
   clothes ( )
   closed ( )

8. **Pronounce:**
   note
   not
   nut

9. **Listen and mark:**
   thick ( )
   tick ( )
   Dick ( )

10. **Pronounce:**
    backed
    bashed
    basked

11. **Listen and mark:**
    mole ( )
    more ( )
    moan ( )

12. **Pronounce:**
    phoned
    fond
    found

13. **Listen and mark:**
    churl ( )
    girl ( )
    whirl ( )

14. **Pronounce:**
    rubber
    rougher
    rudder

15. **Listen and mark:**
    taps ( )
    tapped ( )
    tabs ( )

16. **Pronounce:**
    oil
    owl
    ale

When you finish this exercise, show your page to your partner and compare your answers. Are they the same? Which ones did you miss? Practice pronouncing the words. If you are not sure of the pronunciation, ask your teacher for help. If there is time, do the exercise again, but choose different words to pronounce and make different marks on your page.

Exercise 1.5

Instructions: Pronounce the underlined words for your partner, and listen as your partner pronounces other words for you. If necessary, ask your partner to repeat. Mark an "X" next to the word you hear. Do not look at your partner's page while you are doing this exercise!

1. Pronounce:
ban
van
fan

2. Listen and mark:
piggy ( )
picky ( )
pinky ( )

3. Pronounce:
lagged
lacked
lax

4. Listen and mark:
we ( )
why ( )
weigh ( )

5. Pronounce:
dual
yule
jewel

6. Listen and mark:
witty ( )
witchy ( )
wispy ( )

7. Pronounce:
closed
clothes
clothe

8. Listen and mark:
nut ( )
not ( )
note ( )

9. Pronounce:
Dick
thick
tick

10. Listen and mark:
basked ( )
bashed ( )
backed ( )

11. Pronounce:
mole
moan
more

12. Listen and mark:
found ( )
fond ( )
phoned ( )

13. Pronounce:
churl
whirl
girl

14. Listen and mark:
rougher ( )
rubber ( )
rudder ( )

15. Pronounce:
tapped
tabs
taps

16. Listen and mark:
ale ( )
owl ( )
oil ( )

When you finish this exercise, show your page to your partner and compare your answers. Are they the same? Which ones did you miss? Practice pronouncing the words. If you are not sure of the pronunciation, ask your teacher for help. If there is time, do the exercise again, but choose different words to pronounce and make different marks on your page.

Word List 1.6

Instructions: The following words contain sounds that are difficult for many non-native English speakers to pronounce. Repeat each word after your teacher. Listen carefully to how it is pronounced. Do not worry about the meaning of the words right now. You can look them up in your dictionary later, if you like.

1. sweet
   sheet
   seat

2. holler
   horror
   hotter

3. axe
   axed
   asked

4. dine
   don
   dawn

5. scream
   stream
   scheme

6. teacher
   teether
   teaser

7. peace
   peach
   peas

8. miss
   mace
   mice

9. pay
   play
   pray

10. cup
    cub
    come

11. grid
    grit
    grip

12. heat
    hit
    hate

13. than
    Dan
    tan

14. wined
    wired
    wild

15. cow
    couch
    count

16. even
    Evan
    oven

Exercise 1.6

Instructions: Pronounce the underlined words for your partner, and listen as your partner pronounces other words for you. If necessary, ask your partner to repeat. Mark an "X" next to the word you hear. Do not look at your partner's page while you are doing this exercise!

1. Pronounce:
seat
sweet
sheet

2. Listen and mark:
holler ( )
horror ( )
hotter ( )

3. Pronounce:
asked
axed
axe

4. Listen and mark:
dine ( )
don ( )
dawn ( )

5. Pronounce:
stream
scheme
scream

6. Listen and mark:
teacher ( )
teether ( )
teaser ( )

7. Pronounce:
peach
peace
peas

8. Listen and mark:
miss ( )
mace ( )
mice ( )

9. Pronounce:
pay
pray
play

10. Listen and mark:
cup ( )
cub ( )
come ( )

11. Pronounce:
grip
grid
grit

12. Listen and mark:
heat ( )
hit ( )
hate ( )

13. Pronounce:
tan
Dan
than

14. Listen and mark:
wined ( )
wired ( )
wild ( )

15. Pronounce:
count
couch
cow

16. Listen and mark:
even ( )
Evan ( )
oven ( )

When you finish this exercise, show your page to your partner and compare your answers. Are they the same? Which ones did you miss? Practice pronouncing the words. If you are not sure of the pronunciation, ask your teacher for help. If there is time, do the exercise again, but choose different words to pronounce and make different marks on your page.

Exercise 1.6

Instructions: Pronounce the under-lined words for your partner, and listen as your partner pronounces other words for you. If necessary, ask your partner to repeat. Mark an "X" next to the word you hear. Do not look at your partner's page while you are doing this exercise!

1. Listen and mark:
sweet ( )
sheet ( )
seat ( )

2. Pronounce:
horror
holler
hotter

3. Listen and mark:
axe ( )
axed ( )
asked ( )

4. Pronounce:
don
dawn
dine

5. Listen and mark:
scream ( )
stream ( )
scheme ( )

6. Pronounce:
teaser
teether
teacher

7. Listen and mark:
peace ( )
peach ( )
peas ( )

8. Pronounce:
mace
mice
miss

9. Listen and mark:
pay ( )
play ( )
pray ( )

10. Pronounce:
come
cub
cup

11. Listen and mark:
grid ( )
grit ( )
grip ( )

12. Pronounce:
hate
heat
hit

13. Listen and mark:
than ( )
Dan ( )
tan ( )

14. Pronounce:
wild
wined
wired

15. Listen and mark:
cow ( )
couch ( )
count ( )

16. Pronounce:
even
oven
Evan

When you finish this exercise, show your page to your partner and com-pare your answers. Are they the same? Which ones did you miss? Practice pronouncing the words. If you are not sure of the pronuncia-tion, ask your teacher for help. If there is time, do the exercise again, but choose different words to pro-nounce and make different marks on your page.

Word List 1.7

Instructions: The following words contain sounds that are difficult for many non-native English speakers to pronounce. Repeat each word after your teacher. Listen carefully to how it is pronounced. Do not worry about the meaning of the words right now. You can look them up in your dictionary later, if you like.

1. shrill
   trill
   thrill

2. either
   ether
   eater

3. faith
   fate
   fade

4. boy
   buy
   bay

5. though
   dough
   toe

6. adder
   after
   aster

7. ducks
   ducts
   dusk

8. cat
   cot
   caught

9. drank
   thank
   stank

10. bussing
    budging
    buzzing

11. meant
    mend
    men's

12. hide
    hood
    hoed

13. jot
    yacht
    shot

14. jumble
    jungle
    juggle

15. buds
    buzz
    bud

16. feed
    fad
    fed

Exercise 1.7

Instructions: Pronounce the under-lined words for your partner, and listen as your partner pronounces other words for you. If necessary, ask your partner to repeat. Mark an "X" next to the word you hear. Do not look at your partner's page while you are doing this exercise!

1. **Listen and mark:**
   shrill ( )
   trill ( )
   thrill ( )

2. **Pronounce:**
   eater
   ether
   either

3. **Listen and mark:**
   faith ( )
   fate ( )
   fade ( )

4. **Pronounce:**
   bay
   buy
   boy

5. **Listen and mark:**
   though ( )
   dough ( )
   toe ( )

6. **Pronounce:**
   aster
   after
   adder

7. **Listen and mark:**
   ducks ( )
   ducts ( )
   dusk ( )

8. **Pronounce:**
   cot
   caught
   cat

9. **Listen and mark:**
   drank ( )
   thank ( )
   stank ( )

10. **Pronounce:**
    budging
    buzzing
    bussing

11. **Listen and mark:**
    meant ( )
    mend ( )
    men's ( )

12. **Pronounce:**
    hoed
    hood
    hide

13. **Listen and mark:**
    jot ( )
    yacht ( )
    shot ( )

14. **Pronounce:**
    juggle
    jumble
    jungle

15. **Listen and mark:**
    buds ( )
    bud ( )
    buzz ( )

16. **Pronounce:**
    fed
    fad
    feed

When you finish this exercise, show your page to your partner and com-pare your answers. Are they the same? Which ones did you miss? Practice pronouncing the words. If you are not sure of the pronuncia-tion, ask your teacher for help. If there is time, do the exercise again, but choose different words to pro-nounce and make different marks on your page.

Exercise 1.7

PARTNER

Instructions: Pronounce the underlined words for your partner, and listen as your partner pronounces other words for you. If necessary, ask your partner to repeat. Mark an "X" next to the word you hear. Do not look at your partner's page while you are doing this exercise!

1. Pronounce:
thrill
shrill
trill

2. Listen and mark:
either ( )
ether ( )
eater ( )

3. Pronounce:
fate
faith
fade

4. Listen and mark:
boy ( )
buy ( )
bay ( )

5. Pronounce:
dough
though
toe

6. Listen and mark:
adder ( )
after ( )
aster ( )

7. Pronounce:
ducts
dusk
ducks

8. Listen and mark:
cat ( )
cot ( )
caught ( )

9. Pronounce:
stank
drank
thank

10. Listen and mark:
bussing ( )
budging ( )
buzzing ( )

11. Pronounce:
men's
meant
mend

12. Listen and mark:
hide ( )
hood ( )
hoed ( )

13. Pronounce:
jot
shot
yacht

14. Listen and mark:
jumble ( )
jungle ( )
juggle ( )

15. Pronounce:
buzz
buds
bud

16. Listen and mark:
feed ( )
fad ( )
fed ( )

When you finish this exercise, show your page to your partner and compare your answers. Are they the same? Which ones did you miss? Practice pronouncing the words. If you are not sure of the pronunciation, ask your teacher for help. If there is time, do the exercise again, but choose different words to pronounce and make different marks on your page.

PART ONE / PRONUNCIATION AND AURAL DISCRIMINATION

Word List 1.8

Instructions: The following words contain sounds that are difficult for many non-native English speakers to pronounce. Repeat each word after your teacher. Listen carefully to how it is pronounced. Do not worry about the meaning of the words right now. You can look them up in your dictionary later, if you like.

1. work
   clerk
   Kirk

2. laws
   lawns
   longs

3. lift
   lived
   live

4. fool
   full
   foal

5. peasant
   pleasant
   present

6. trainer
   trader
   trailer

7. force
   fourth
   fours

8. bitter
   better
   batter

9. fame
   flame
   frame

10. hitting
    hissing
    hitching

11. host
    hose
    hosed

12. knit
    net
    gnat

13. sty
    spy
    spry

14. muscle
    muzzle
    muddle

15. ants
    and
    Ann's

16. pick
    pack
    peck

Exercise 1.8

Instructions: Pronounce the underlined words for your partner, and listen as your partner pronounces other words for you. If necessary, ask your partner to repeat. Mark an "X" next to the word you hear. Do not look at your partner's page while you are doing this exercise!

1. Pronounce:
Kirk
clerk
work

2. Listen and mark:
laws ( )
lawns ( )
longs ( )

3. Pronounce:
lift
live
lived

4. Listen and mark:
fool ( )
full ( )
foal ( )

5. Pronounce:
pleasant
peasant
present

6. Listen and mark:
trainer ( )
trader ( )
trailer ( )

7. Pronounce:
force
fours
fourth

8. Listen and mark:
bitter ( )
better ( )
batter ( )

9. Pronounce:
frame
flame
fame

10. Listen and mark:
hitting ( )
hissing ( )
hitching ( )

11. Pronounce:
host
hosed
hose

12. Listen and mark:
knit ( )
net ( )
gnat ( )

13. Pronounce:
sty
spry
spy

14. Listen and mark:
muscle ( )
muzzle ( )
muddle ( )

15. Pronounce:
ants
Ann's
and

16. Listen and mark:
pick ( )
pack ( )
peck ( )

When you finish this exercise, show your page to your partner and compare your answers. Are they the same? Which ones did you miss? Practice pronouncing the words. If you are not sure of the pronunciation, ask your teacher for help. If there is time, do the exercise again, but choose different words to pronounce and make different marks on your page.

Exercise 1.8

Instructions: Pronounce the underlined words for your partner, and listen as your partner pronounces other words for you. If necessary, ask your partner to repeat. Mark an "X" next to the word you hear. Do not look at your partner's page while you are doing this exercise!

1. Listen and mark:
work   (   )
clerk   (   )
Kirk   (   )

2. Pronounce:
longs
lawns
laws

3. Listen and mark:
lift   (   )
lived   (   )
live   (   )

4. Pronounce:
fool
foal
full

5. Listen and mark:
peasant   (   )
pleasant   (   )
present   (   )

6. Pronounce:
trailer
trainer
trader

7. Listen and mark:
force   (   )
fourth   (   )
fours   (   )

8. Pronounce:
batter
better
bitter

9. Listen and mark:
fame   (   )
flame   (   )
frame   (   )

10. Pronounce:
hissing
hitching
hitting

11. Listen and mark:
host   (   )
hose   (   )
hosed   (   )

12. Pronounce:
gnat
knit
net

13. Listen and mark:
sty   (   )
spy   (   )
spry   (   )

14. Pronounce:
muzzle
muscle
muddle

15. Listen and mark:
ants   (   )
and   (   )
Ann's   (   )

16. Pronounce:
peck
pack
pick

When you finish this exercise, show your page to your partner and compare your answers. Are they the same? Which ones did you miss? Practice pronouncing the words. If you are not sure of the pronunciation, ask your teacher for help. If there is time, do the exercise again, but choose different words to pronounce and make different marks on your page.

PART TWO
DESCRIBING A PICTURE

To the Teacher

PART TWO
DESCRIBING
A PICTURE

1. The object of this activity, and of the following one, is to present students with a communication challenge. In Part Two, students use whatever language is available to them to describe a particular picture for their partner to identify. As in Part One, students are not to look at each other's pages.

   Some teachers present the activity without prior classroom preparation and without the use of dictionaries. After everyone has performed the activity once, the teacher answers questions about the pictures. The students then regroup with new partners, exchange papers, and repeat the activity.

   You may prefer, however, to prepare students by giving them some vocabulary that will be useful in describing the pictures. Although such preparation is not necessary for performance of the activity, some vocabulary can be incorporated into lessons beforehand. Word lists can be posted in the classroom. Be careful, though, that you don't remove the challenge by allowing students to write or copy the words onto the pictures themselves. The descriptions should be as spontaneous and as varied as possible, and students should be discouraged from using set grammatical patterns. There is no one "right" way to describe any picture.

2. Here are some words associated with the pictures in Part Two.

   Exercise 1: square, rectangle; hexagonal, oblong, round, oval; basket; collar, sleeve; throw, kick

   Exercise 2: club (card suit), sideways; crossed arms, elbow(s), hips

   Exercise 3: pendulum, face and hands of a clock; chest of drawers; circle, intersecting lines; pull, tug

   Exercise 4: parallel bars; horizontal, vertical; mug, bottle; squares, triangles

   Exercise 5: crooked, straight; football, baseball, basketball, beach ball; bald, moustache, sideburns; rectangles, squares

   Exercise 6: leash; numerals, words; stack, rectangle

   Exercise 7: bow, brim of a hat, hatband; pot, handle; frames of glasses; circle, triangle, pointed

   Exercise 8: stars, ovals; upside down; fractions; exercise bar

Sample Exercise 2

The exercises in Part Two will give you practice in using and understanding language used in description.

WHAT TO DO

You and your partner will each receive an exercise page. On each page there will be pictures for you to describe and choices for you to make. Look at example 1, below. The picture at the left, with the black dot (●) in the corner, is the one to be described.

1. If you are Partner A, describe:

2. If you are Partner B, listen and mark:

The correct choice is marked "X." Now do example 2. This time Partner B will describe the picture. Partner A will listen and mark the answer.

2. If you are Partner A, listen and mark:

If you are Partner B, describe:

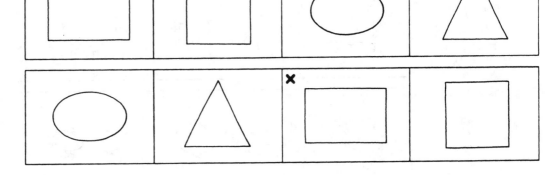

When you finish an exercise, review your answers with your partner. Be sure to discuss your mistakes and any problems you had. Then repeat the exercise with the same partner (exchange papers) or with a different partner, and choose different pictures. Mark your answers with a new mark (✔).

Exercise 2.1

Instructions: Describe the indicated pictures (●) to your partner, and listen as your partner describes other pictures to you. Mark (X) the picture described. Do not look at your partner's page while you are doing this exercise!

1. Describe.

2. Listen and mark.

3. Describe.

4. Listen and mark.

5. Describe.

6. Listen and mark.

When you finish this exercise, show your page to your partner and compare your answers. Are they all the same? Which ones did you miss? If there is time, do the exercise again, but choose different pictures to describe and make different marks on your page.

Exercise 2.1

Instructions: Describe the indicated pictures (●) to your partner, and listen as your partner describes other pictures to you. Mark (X) the picture described. Do not look at your partner's page while you are doing this exercise!

1. Listen and mark.

2. Describe.

3. Listen and mark.

4. Describe.

5. Listen and mark.

6. Describe.

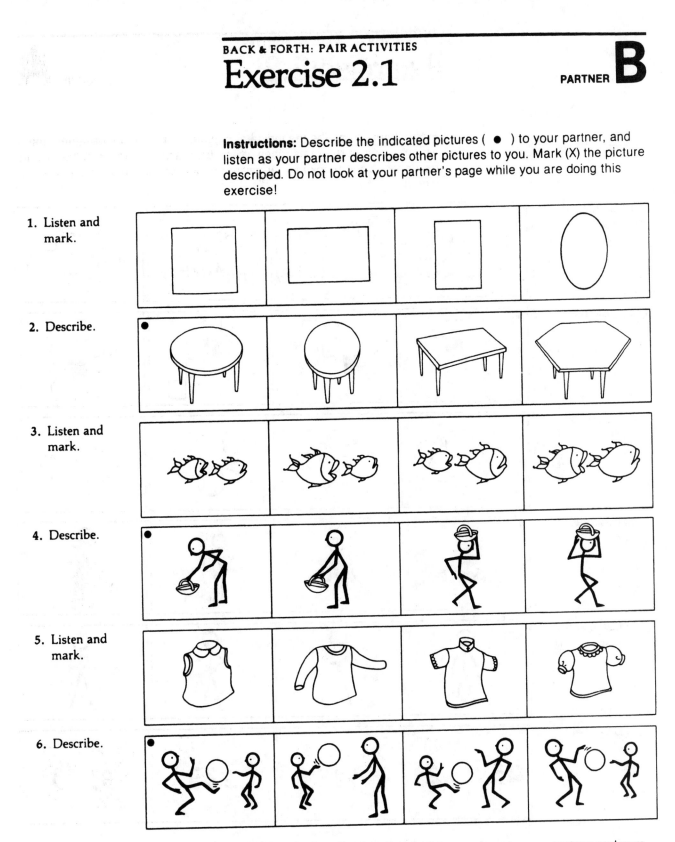

When you finish this exercise, show your page to your partner and compare your answers. Are they all the same? Which ones did you miss? If there is time, do the exercise again, but choose different pictures to describe and make different marks on your page.

Exercise 2.2

Instructions: Describe the indicated pictures (●) to your partner, and listen as your partner describes other pictures to you. Mark (X) the picture described. Do not look at your partner's page while you are doing this exercise!

1. Listen and mark.

2. Describe.

3. Listen and mark.

4. Describe.

5. Listen and mark.

6. Describe.

When you finish this exercise, show your page to your partner and compare your answers. Are they all the same? Which ones did you miss? If there is time, do the exercise again, but choose different pictures to describe and make different marks on your page.

Exercise 2.2

Instructions: Describe the indicated pictures (●) to your partner, and listen as your partner describes other pictures to you. Mark (X) the picture described. Do not look at your partner's page while you are doing this exercise!

1. Describe.

2. Listen and mark.

3. Describe.

4. Listen and mark.

5. Describe.

6. Listen and mark.

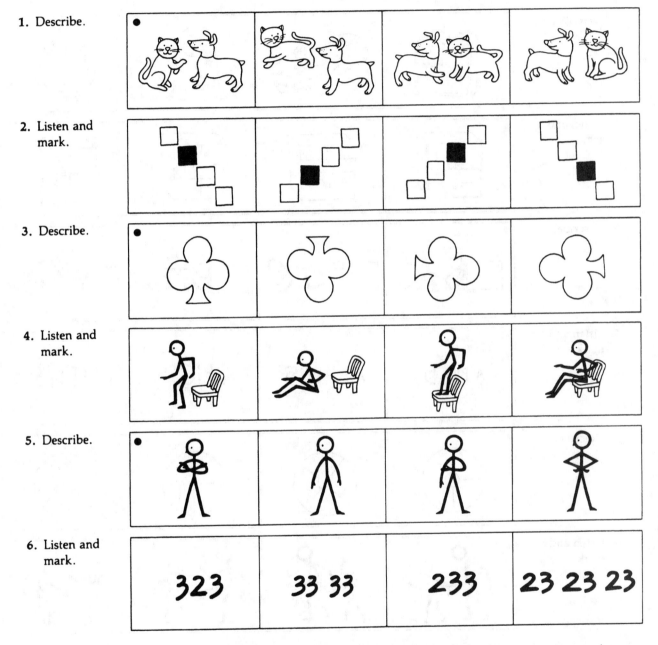

When you finish this exercise, show your page to your partner and compare your answers. Are they all the same? Which ones did you miss? If there is time, do the exercise again, but choose different pictures to describe and make different marks on your page.

Exercise 2.3

PARTNER  A

Instructions: Describe the indicated pictures (●) to your partner, and listen as your partner describes other pictures to you. Mark (X) the picture described. Do not look at your partner's page while you are doing this exercise!

1. Describe.

2. Listen and mark.

3. Describe.

4. Listen and mark.

5. Describe.

6. Listen and mark.

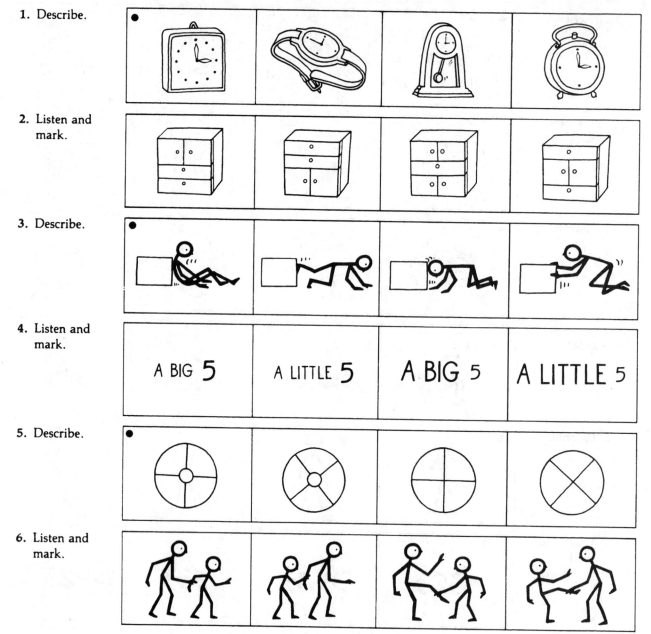

When you finish this exercise, show your page to your partner and compare your answers. Are they all the same? Which ones did you miss? If there is time, do the exercise again, but choose different pictures to describe and make different marks on your page.

Exercise 2.3

Instructions: Describe the indicated pictures (●) to your partner, and listen as your partner describes other pictures to you. Mark (X) the picture described. Do not look at your partner's page while you are doing this exercise!

1. Listen and mark.

2. Describe.

3. Listen and mark.

4. Describe.

5. Listen and mark.

6. Describe.

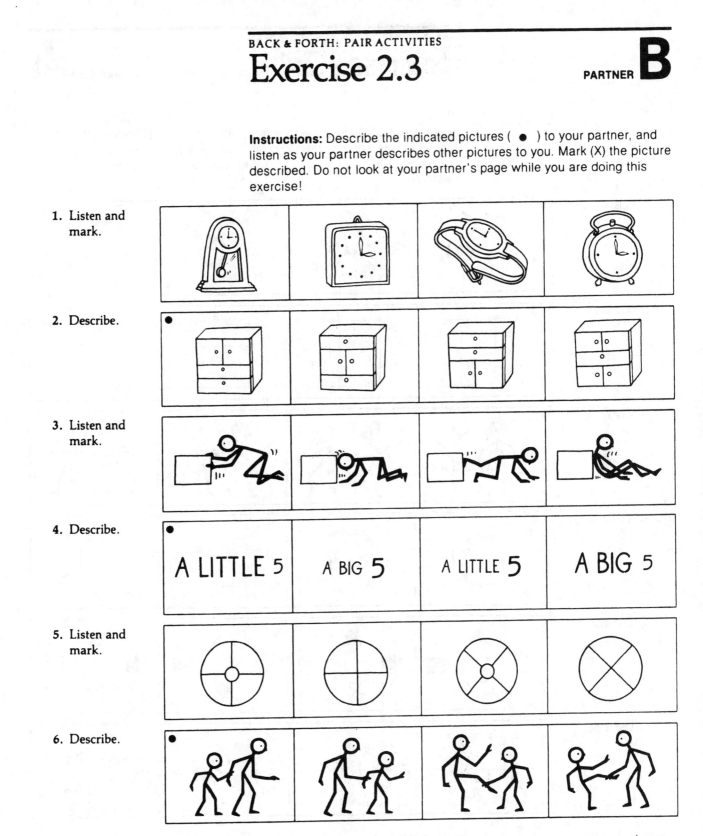

When you finish this exercise, show your page to your partner and compare your answers. Are they all the same? Which ones did you miss? If there is time, do the exercise again, but choose different pictures to describe and make different marks on your page.

Exercise 2.4

Instructions: Describe the indicated pictures (●) to your partner, and listen as your partner describes other pictures to you. Mark (X) the picture described. Do not look at your partner's page while you are doing this exercise!

1. Listen and mark.

2. Describe.

3. Listen and mark.

4. Describe.

5. Listen and mark.

6. Describe.

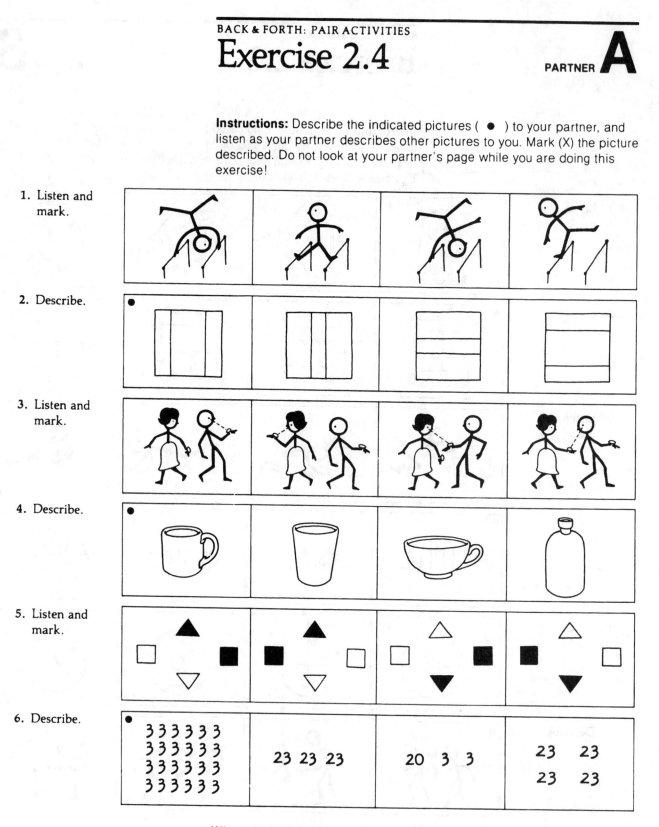

When you finish this exercise, show your page to your partner and compare your answers. Are they all the same? Which ones did you miss? If there is time, do the exercise again, but choose different pictures to describe and make different marks on your page.

Exercise 2.4

Instructions: Describe the indicated pictures (●) to your partner, and listen as your partner describes other pictures to you. Mark (X) the picture described. Do not look at your partner's page while you are doing this exercise!

1. Describe.

2. Listen and mark.

3. Describe.

4. Listen and mark.

5. Describe.

6. Listen and mark.

| 20 3 3 | 3 3 3 3 3 3
3 3 3 3 3 3
3 3 3 3 3 3
3 3 3 3 3 3 | 23   23

23   23 | 23 23 23 |

When you finish this exercise, show your page to your partner and compare your answers. Are they all the same? Which ones did you miss? If there is time, do the exercise again, but choose different pictures to describe and make different marks on your page.

Exercise 2.5

Instructions: Describe the indicated pictures (●) to your partner, and listen as your partner describes other pictures to you. Mark (X) the picture described. Do not look at your partner's page while you are doing this exercise!

1. Describe.

2. Listen and mark.

3. Describe.

4. Listen and mark.

5. Describe.

6. Listen and mark.

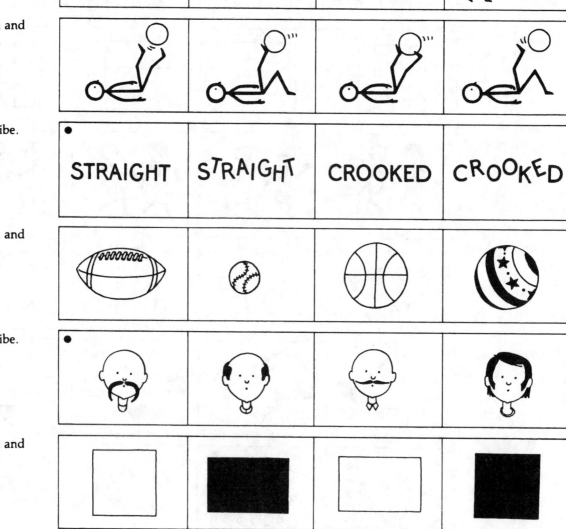

When you finish this exercise, show your page to your partner and compare your answers. Are they all the same? Which ones did you miss? If there is time, do the exercise again, but choose different pictures to describe and make different marks on your page.

Exercise 2.5

Instructions: Describe the indicated pictures (●) to your partner, and listen as your partner describes other pictures to you. Mark (X) the picture described. Do not look at your partner's page while you are doing this exercise!

1. Listen and mark.

2. Describe.

3. Listen and mark.

| STRAIGHT | STRAIGHT | CROOKED | CROOKED |

4. Describe.

5. Listen and mark.

6. Describe.

When you finish this exercise, show your page to your partner and compare your answers. Are they all the same? Which ones did you miss? If there is time, do the exercise again, but choose different pictures to describe and make different marks on your page.

Exercise 2.6

Instructions: Describe the indicated pictures (●) to your partner, and listen as your partner describes other pictures to you. Mark (X) the picture described. Do not look at your partner's page while you are doing this exercise!

1. Listen and mark.

2. Describe.

3. Listen and mark.

4. Describe.

5. Listen and mark.

6. Describe.

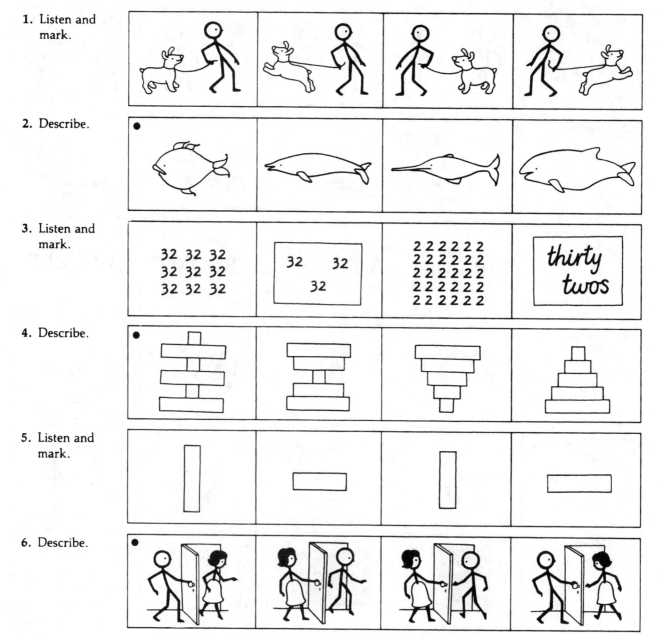

When you finish this exercise, show your page to your partner and compare your answers. Are they all the same? Which ones did you miss? If there is time, do the exercise again, but choose different pictures to describe and make different marks on your page.

Exercise 2.6

Instructions: Describe the indicated pictures (●) to your partner, and listen as your partner describes other pictures to you. Mark (X) the picture described. Do not look at your partner's page while you are doing this exercise!

1. Describe.

2. Listen and mark.

3. Describe.

4. Listen and mark.

5. Describe.

6. Listen and mark.

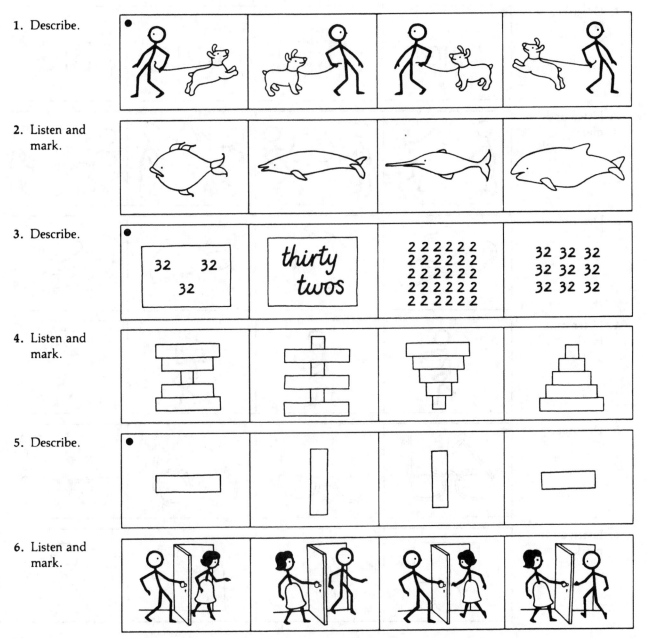

When you finish this exercise, show your page to your partner and compare your answers. Are they all the same? Which ones did you miss? If there is time, do the exercise again, but choose different pictures to describe and make different marks on your page.

Exercise 2.7

Instructions: Describe the indicated pictures (●) to your partner, and listen as your partner describes other pictures to you. Mark (X) the picture described. Do not look at your partner's page while you are doing this exercise!

1. Describe.

2. Listen and mark.

3. Describe.

4. Listen and mark.

5. Describe.

6. Listen and mark.

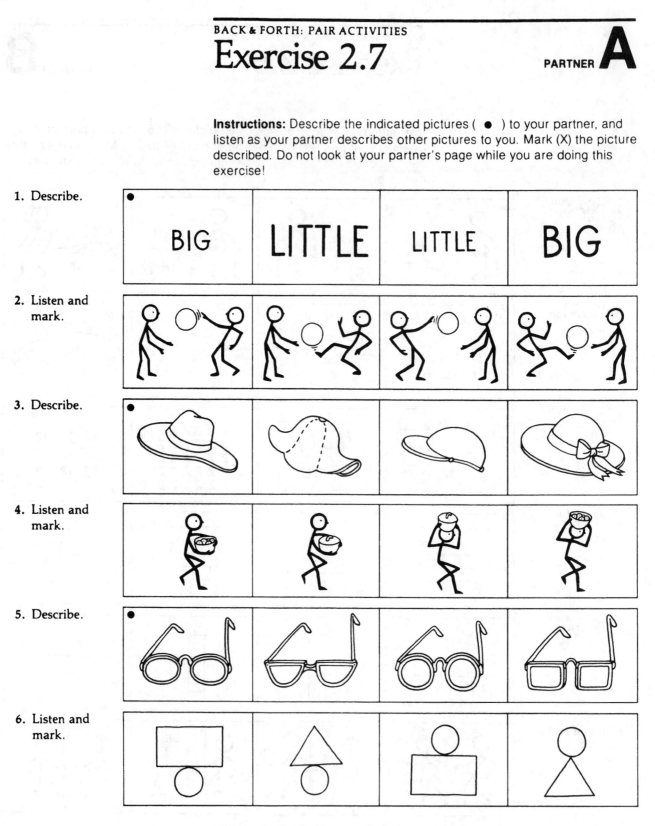

When you finish this exercise, show your page to your partner and compare your answers. Are they all the same? Which ones did you miss? If there is time, do the exercise again, but choose different pictures to describe and make different marks on your page.

Exercise 2.7

PARTNER **B**

Instructions: Describe the indicated pictures (●) to your partner, and listen as your partner describes other pictures to you. Mark (X) the picture described. Do not look at your partner's page while you are doing this exercise!

1. Listen and mark.

2. Describe.

3. Listen and mark.

4. Describe.

5. Listen and mark.

6. Describe.

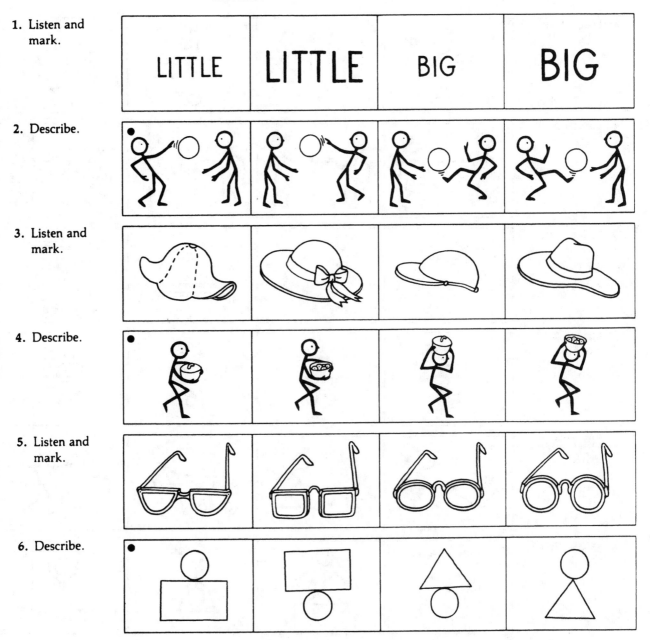

When you finish this exercise, show your page to your partner and compare your answers. Are they all the same? Which ones did you miss? If there is time, do the exercise again, but choose different pictures to describe and make different marks on your page.

Exercise 2.8

Instructions: Describe the indicated pictures (●) to your partner, and listen as your partner describes other pictures to you. Mark (X) the picture described. Do not look at your partner's page while you are doing this exercise!

1. Listen and mark.

2. Describe.

3. Listen and mark.

4. Describe.

5. Listen and mark.

6. Describe.

When you finish this exercise, show your page to your partner and compare your answers. Are they all the same? Which ones did you miss? If there is time, do the exercise again, but choose different pictures to describe and make different marks on your page.

Exercise 2.8

Instructions: Describe the indicated pictures (●) to your partner, and listen as your partner describes other pictures to you. Mark (X) the picture described. Do not look at your partner's page while you are doing this exercise!

1. Describe.

2. Listen and mark.

3. Describe.

4. Listen and mark.

5. Describe.

6. Listen and mark.

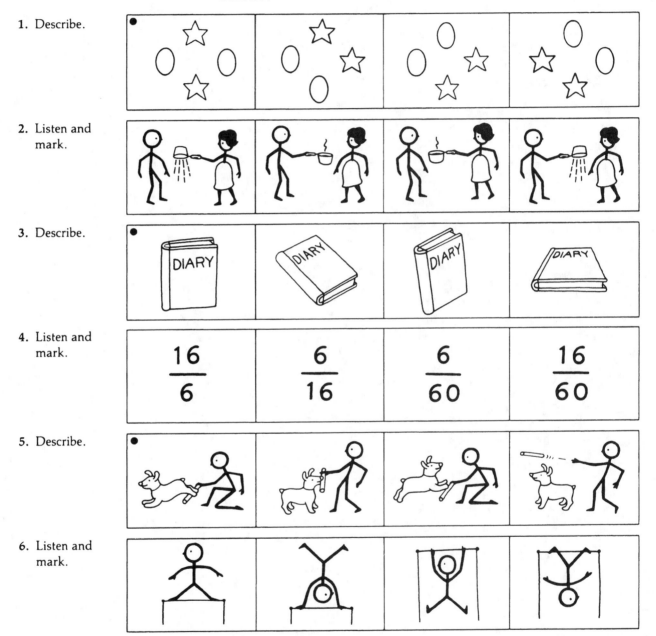

When you finish this exercise, show your page to your partner and compare your answers. Are they all the same? Which ones did you miss? If there is time, do the exercise again, but choose different pictures to describe and make different marks on your page.

PART THREE

ASKING AND ANSWERING QUESTIONS ABOUT A PICTURE

To the Teacher

1. The communication challenge in Part Three is for students to ask questions of their partners so that they are able to correctly identify a picture. Questions that ask for information, such as "Is the man sitting or standing?" or "Does the figure have three sides?" are appropriate. Questions that require a full description, such as "What is the man doing?" or "Which picture is it?" are not. Again, students should not look at each other's pages.

2. After students have completed the activity using the pictures in Part Three, they can repeat it using the pictures in Part Two.

3. The following vocabulary can be useful to students in asking and answering questions about the pictures. Remember, however, that students need not know all these words in order to perform the activity. Practice in finding other ways to talk about the pictures may be more helpful to students whose vocabulary is limited.

    Exercise 1: box, lift; cans, horizontal, vertical; sail, mast; dish, leaf, vase; hold, linked arms

    Exercise 2: exercise bar, hang, upside down; curvy, straight, horizontal, vertical; point, kneel; purse (handbag), handle; curly, pigtails

    Exercise 3: rounded; flag; neck, shoulder; glass, pour, vase; kite, string, diamond, star, dove

    Exercise 4: handles, vase; oval, horizontal, vertical; kick, catch; point, kneel; pour, spill, pot, glass; arms of a chair

    Exercise 5: heart, spade, diamond, club (card suits); barbells, weights, lift; rounded, arch; arabic and roman numerals, face and hands of a clock

    Exercise 6: umbrella; doorknob, keyhole, key, lock; point; rectangle, circle, triangle, square; beard, moustache, goatee

    Exercise 7: rounded, pointed; crossed, ankles; bouncing; lampshade, base of a lamp; curtains, rod, drapes

    Exercise 8: sleeves, pocket, collar; cart, push, pull; oval, rectangle; pan, lid

Sample Exercise 3

The exercises in Part Three will give you practice in asking questions and giving answers that will help in identifying pictures.

WHAT TO DO

You and your partner will each receive an exercise page. On each page there will be pictures for you to identify by asking your partner questions. You will also answer questions from your partner about other pictures. Look at example 1, below. The picture at the left, with the black dot (●) in the corner, is the one to be identified.

1. **If you are Partner A, ask and mark:**

BIG	LITTLE	✗ LITTLE	BIG

 If you are Partner B, answer:

● LITTLE	LITTLE	BIG	BIG

The correct choice is marked "X." Now do example 2. This time Partner A will identify the picture. Partner B will ask questions and mark the answer.

2. **If you are Partner A, answer:**

 If you are Partner B, ask and mark:

When you finish an exercise, review your answers with your partner. Be sure to discuss your mistakes and any problems you had. Then repeat the exercise with the same partner (exchange papers) or with a different partner, and choose different pictures. Mark your answers with a new mark (✔).

Exercise 3.1

Instructions: Listen and answer as your partner asks questions about the pictures on your page. Ask questions about the pictures on your partner's page. Mark (X) the picture you think is indicated (●) on your partner's page. Do not look at your partner's page while you are doing this exercise!

1. Listen and answer.

2. Ask and mark.

3. Listen and answer.

4. Ask and mark.

5. Listen and answer.

6. Ask and mark.

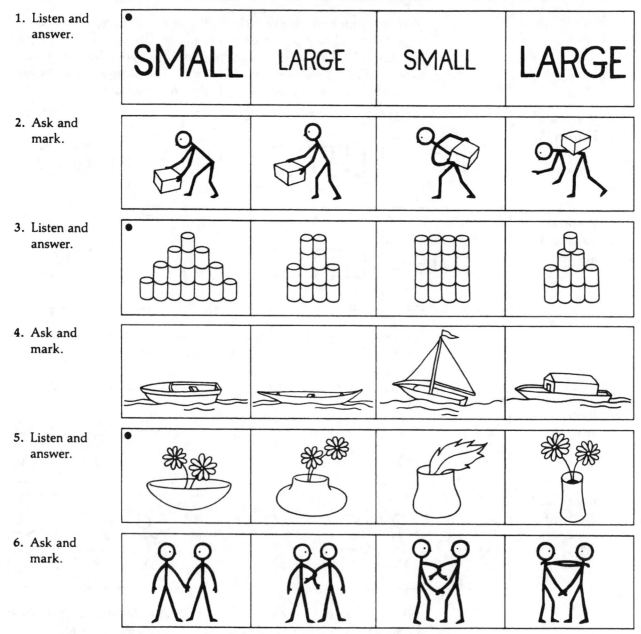

When you finish this exercise, show your page to your partner and compare your answers. Are they all the same? Which ones did you miss? If there is time, do the exercise again, but choose different pictures to ask questions about and make different marks on your page.

Exercise 3.1

Instructions: Listen and answer as your partner asks questions about the pictures on your page. Ask questions about the pictures on your partner's page. Mark (X) the picture you think is indicated (●) on your partner's page. Do not look at your partner's page while you are doing this exercise!

1. Ask and mark.
2. Listen and answer.
3. Ask and mark.
4. Listen and answer.
5. Ask and mark.
6. Listen and answer.

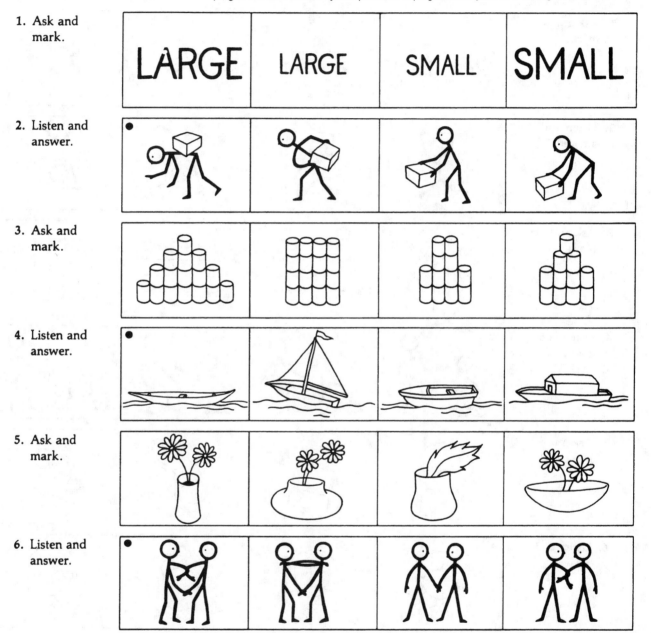

When you finish this exercise, show your page to your partner and compare your answers. Are they all the same? Which ones did you miss? If there is time, do the exercise again, but choose different pictures to ask questions about and make different marks on your page.

Exercise 3.2

PARTNER

Instructions: Listen and answer as your partner asks questions about the pictures on your page. Ask questions about the pictures on your partner's page. Mark (X) the picture you think is indicated (●) on your partner's page. Do not look at your partner's page while you are doing this exercise!

1. Ask and mark.

2. Listen and answer.

3. Ask and mark.

4. Listen and answer.

5. Ask and mark.

6. Listen and answer.

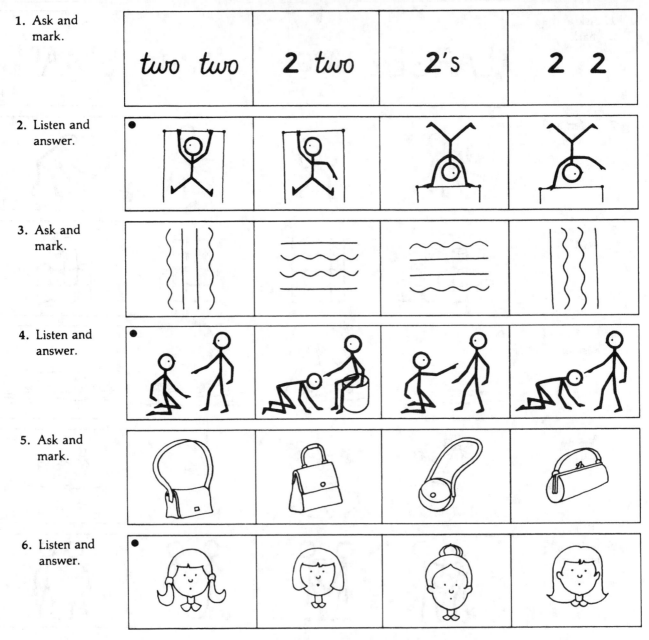

When you finish this exercise, show your page to your partner and compare your answers. Are they all the same? Which ones did you miss? If there is time, do the exercise again, but choose different pictures to ask questions about and make different marks on your page.

Exercise 3.2

Instructions: Listen and answer as your partner asks questions about the pictures on your page. Ask questions about the pictures on your partner's page. Mark (X) the picture you think is indicated (●) on your partner's page. Do not look at your partner's page while you are doing this exercise!

1. Listen and answer.

● *2 two*	*2's*	*two two*	*2 2*

2. Ask and mark.

3. Listen and answer.

4. Ask and mark.

5. Listen and answer.

6. Ask and mark.

When you finish this exercise, show your page to your partner and compare your answers. Are they all the same? Which ones did you miss? If there is time, do the exercise again, but choose different pictures to ask questions about and make different marks on your page.

Exercise 3.3

Instructions: Listen and answer as your partner asks questions about the pictures on your page. Ask questions about the pictures on your partner's page. Mark (X) the picture you think is indicated (●) on your partner's page. Do not look at your partner's page while you are doing this exercise!

1. Ask and mark.

2. Listen and answer.

3. Ask and mark.

4. Listen and answer.

5. Ask and mark.

6. Listen and answer.

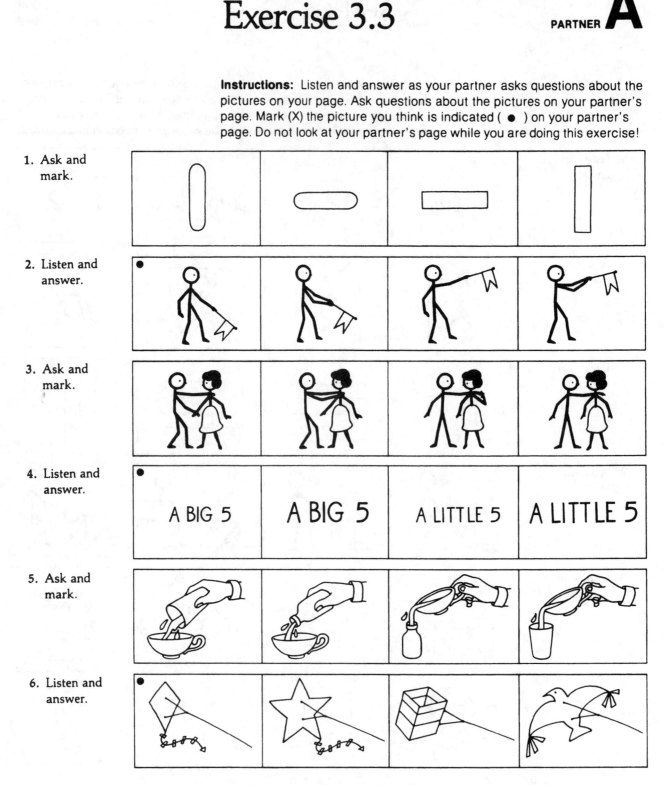

When you finish this exercise, show your page to your partner and compare your answers. Are they all the same? Which ones did you miss? If there is time, do the exercise again, but choose different pictures to ask questions about and make different marks on your page.

Exercise 3.3

Instructions: Listen and answer as your partner asks questions about the pictures on your page. Ask questions about the pictures on your partner's page. Mark (X) the picture you think is indicated (●) on your partner's page. Do not look at your partner's page while you are doing this exercise!

1. Listen and answer.

2. Ask and mark.

3. Listen and answer.

4. Ask and mark.

5. Listen and answer.

6. Ask and mark.

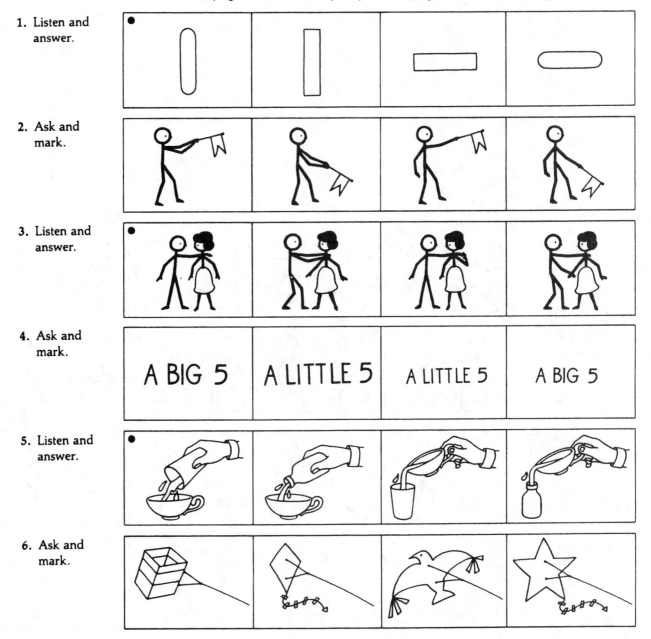

When you finish this exercise, show your page to your partner and compare your answers. Are they all the same? Which ones did you miss? If there is time, do the exercise again, but choose different pictures to ask questions about and make different marks on your page.

Exercise 3.4

Instructions: Listen and answer as your partner asks questions about the pictures on your page. Ask questions about the pictures on your partner's page. Mark (X) the picture you think is indicated (●) on your partner's page. Do not look at your partner's page while you are doing this exercise!

1. Ask and mark.

2. Listen and answer.

3. Ask and mark.

4. Listen and answer.

5. Ask and mark.

6. Listen and answer.

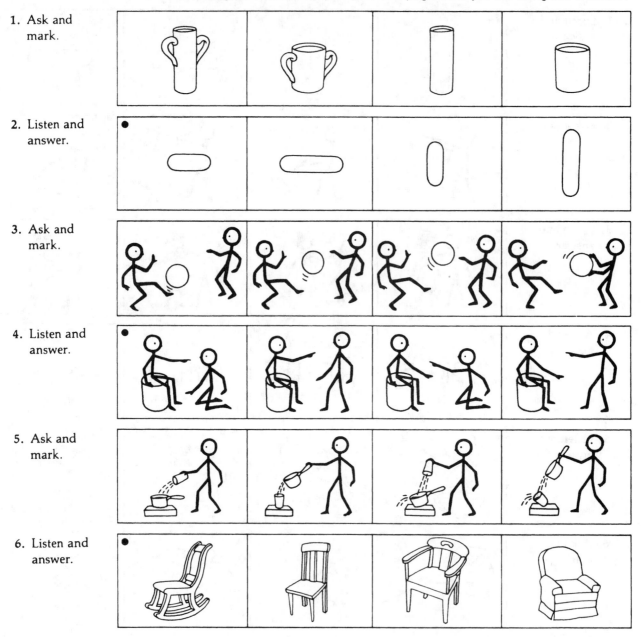

When you finish this exercise, show your page to your partner and compare your answers. Are they all the same? Which ones did you miss? If there is time, do the exercise again, but choose different pictures to ask questions about and make different marks on your page.

Exercise 3.4

Instructions: Listen and answer as your partner asks questions about the pictures on your page. Ask questions about the pictures on your partner's page. Mark (X) the picture you think is indicated (●) on your partner's page. Do not look at your partner's page while you are doing this exercise!

1. Listen and answer.

2. Ask and mark.

3. Listen and answer.

4. Ask and mark.

5. Listen and answer.

6. Ask and mark.

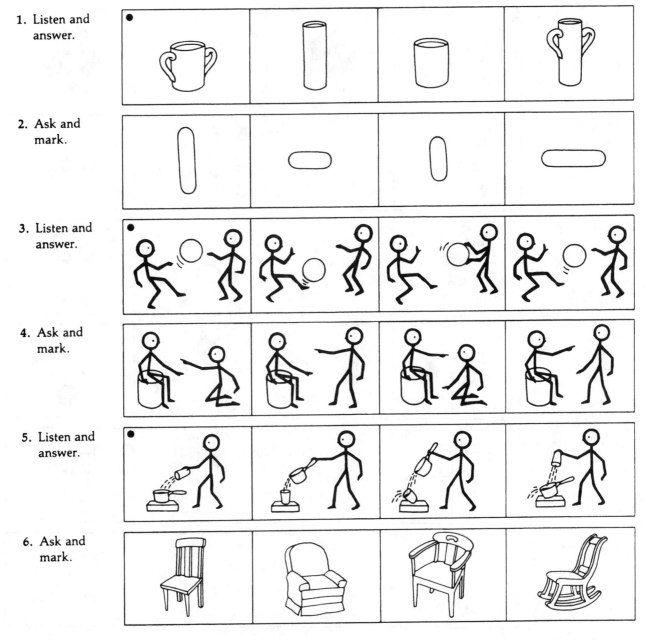

When you finish this exercise, show your page to your partner and compare your answers. Are they all the same? Which ones did you miss? If there is time, do the exercise again, but choose different pictures to ask questions about and make different marks on your page.

Exercise 3.5

Instructions: Listen and answer as your partner asks questions about the pictures on your page. Ask questions about the pictures on your partner's page. Mark (X) the picture you think is indicated (●) on your partner's page. Do not look at your partner's page while you are doing this exercise!

1. Listen and answer.

2. Ask and mark.

3. Listen and answer.

4. Ask and mark.

5. Listen and answer.

6. Ask and mark.

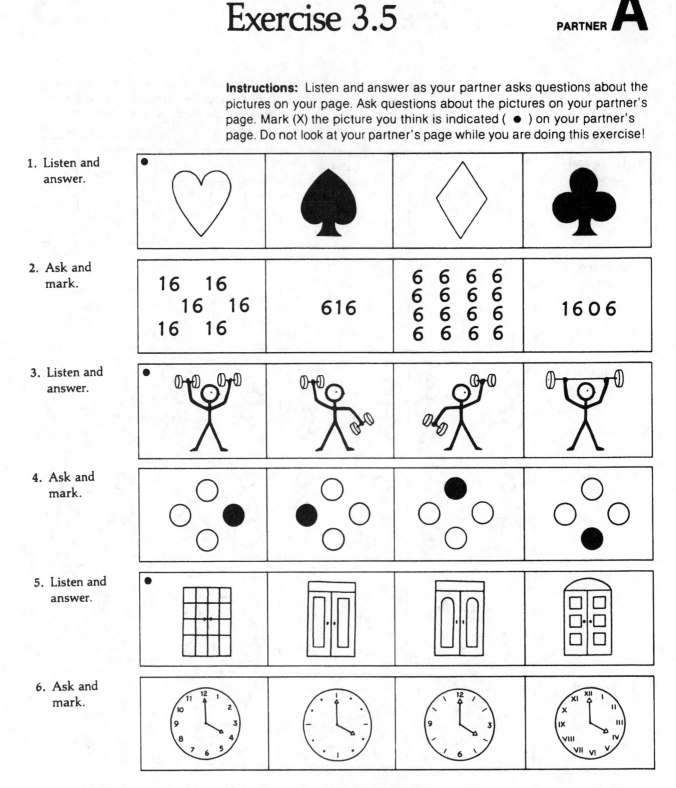

When you finish this exercise, show your page to your partner and compare your answers. Are they all the same? Which ones did you miss? If there is time, do the exercise again, but choose different pictures to ask questions about and make different marks on your page.

Exercise 3.5

Instructions: Listen and answer as your partner asks questions about the pictures on your page. Ask questions about the pictures on your partner's page. Mark (X) the picture you think is indicated (●) on your partner's page. Do not look at your partner's page while you are doing this exercise!

1. Ask and mark.

2. Listen and answer.

16 16 16 16 16 16	6 6 6 6 6 6 6 6 6 6 6 6 6 6 6 6	616	16 0 6

3. Ask and mark.

4. Listen and answer.

5. Ask and mark.

6. Listen and answer.

When you finish this exercise, show your page to your partner and compare your answers. Are they all the same? Which ones did you miss? If there is time, do the exercise again, but choose different pictures to ask questions about and make different marks on your page.

Exercise 3.6

Instructions: Listen and answer as your partner asks questions about the pictures on your page. Ask questions about the pictures on your partner's page. Mark (X) the picture you think is indicated (●) on your partner's page. Do not look at your partner's page while you are doing this exercise!

1. Ask and mark.

2. Listen and answer.

3. Ask and mark.

4. Listen and answer.

5. Ask and mark.

6. Listen and answer.

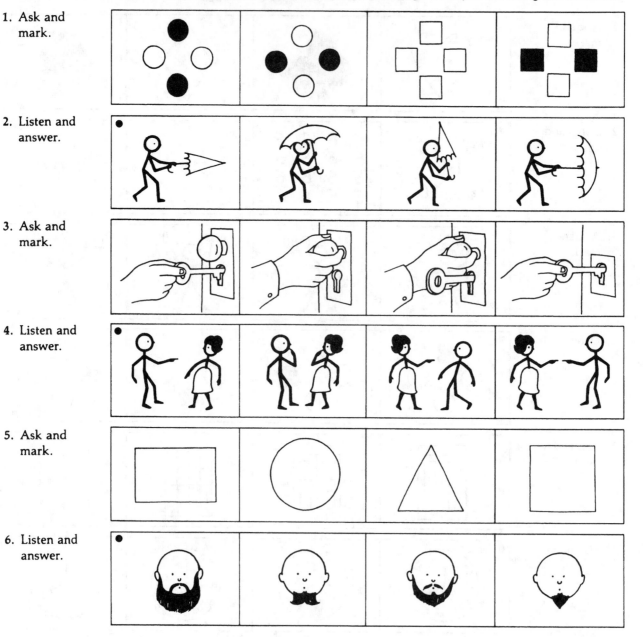

When you finish this exercise, show your page to your partner and compare your answers. Are they all the same? Which ones did you miss? If there is time, do the exercise again, but choose different pictures to ask questions about and make different marks on your page.

Exercise 3.6

Instructions: Listen and answer as your partner asks questions about the pictures on your page. Ask questions about the pictures on your partner's page. Mark (X) the picture you think is indicated (●) on your partner's page. Do not look at your partner's page while you are doing this exercise!

1. Listen and answer.

2. Ask and mark.

3. Listen and answer.

4. Ask and mark.

5. Listen and answer.

6. Ask and mark.

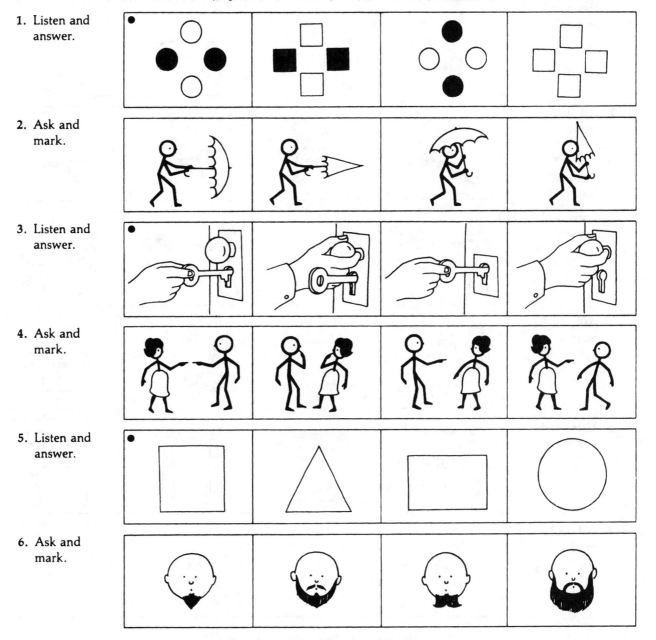

When you finish this exercise, show your page to your partner and compare your answers. Are they all the same? Which ones did you miss? If there is time, do the exercise again, but choose different pictures to ask questions about and make different marks on your page.

Exercise 3.7

Instructions: Listen and answer as your partner asks questions about the pictures on your page. Ask questions about the pictures on your partner's page. Mark (X) the picture you think is indicated (●) on your partner's page. Do not look at your partner's page while you are doing this exercise!

1. Listen and answer.

2. Ask and mark.

3. Listen and answer.

4. Ask and mark.

5. Listen and answer.

6. Ask and mark.

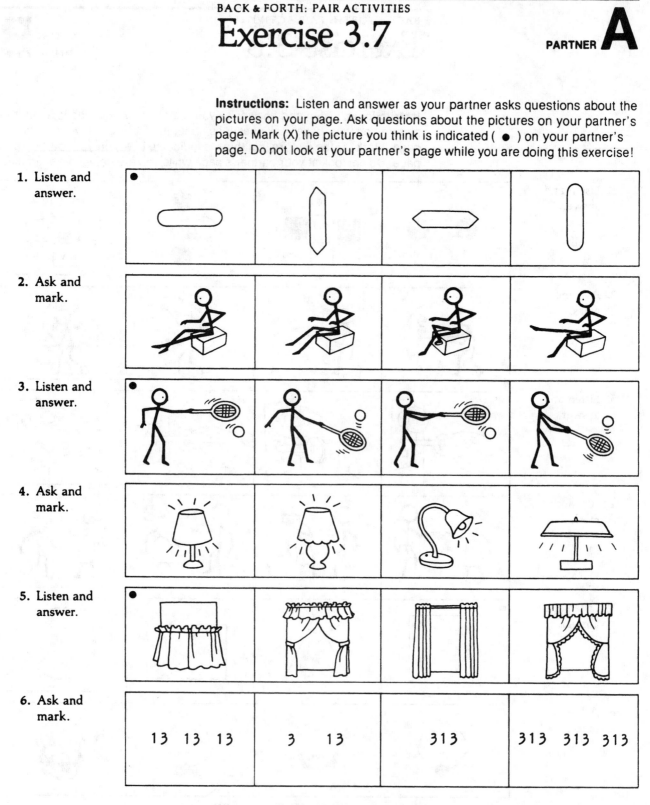

13 13 13	3 13	3 1 3	3 1 3 3 1 3 3 1 3

When you finish this exercise, show your page to your partner and compare your answers. Are they all the same? Which ones did you miss? If there is time, do the exercise again, but choose different pictures to ask questions about and make different marks on your page.

Exercise 3.7

Instructions: Listen and answer as your partner asks questions about the pictures on your page. Ask questions about the pictures on your partner's page. Mark (X) the picture you think is indicated (●) on your partner's page. Do not look at your partner's page while you are doing this exercise!

1. Ask and mark.

2. Listen and answer.

3. Ask and mark.

4. Listen and answer.

5. Ask and mark.

6. Listen and answer.

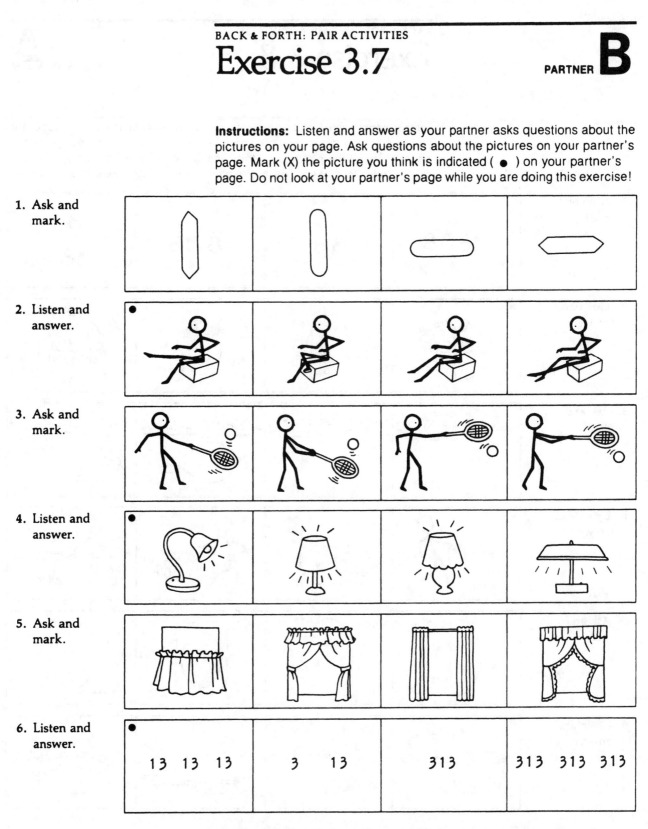

When you finish this exercise, show your page to your partner and compare your answers. Are they all the same? Which ones did you miss? If there is time, do the exercise again, but choose different pictures to ask questions about and make different marks on your page.

Exercise 3.8

Instructions: Listen and answer as your partner asks questions about the pictures on your page. Ask questions about the pictures on your partner's page. Mark (X) the picture you think is indicated (●) on your partner's page. Do not look at your partner's page while you are doing this exercise!

1. Ask and mark.

2. Listen and answer.

3. Ask and mark.

4. Listen and answer.

5. Ask and mark.

6. Listen and answer.

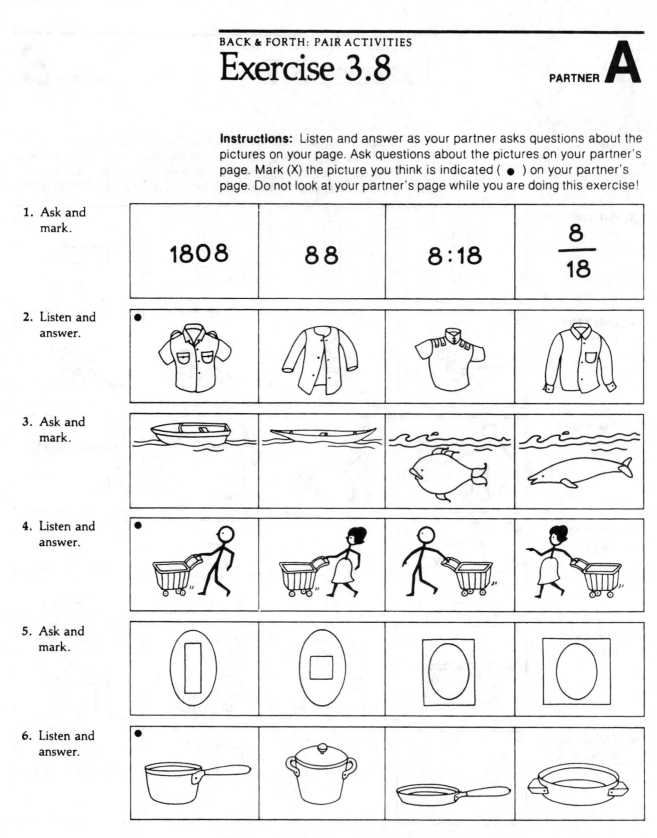

When you finish this exercise, show your page to your partner and compare your answers. Are they all the same? Which ones did you miss? If there is time, do the exercise again, but choose different pictures to ask questions about and make different marks on your page.

Exercise 3.8

Instructions: Listen and answer as your partner asks questions about the pictures on your page. Ask questions about the pictures on your partner's page. Mark (X) the picture you think is indicated (●) on your partner's page. Do not look at your partner's page while you are doing this exercise!

1. Listen and answer.

2. Ask and mark.

3. Listen and answer.

4. Ask and mark.

5. Listen and answer.

6. Ask and mark.

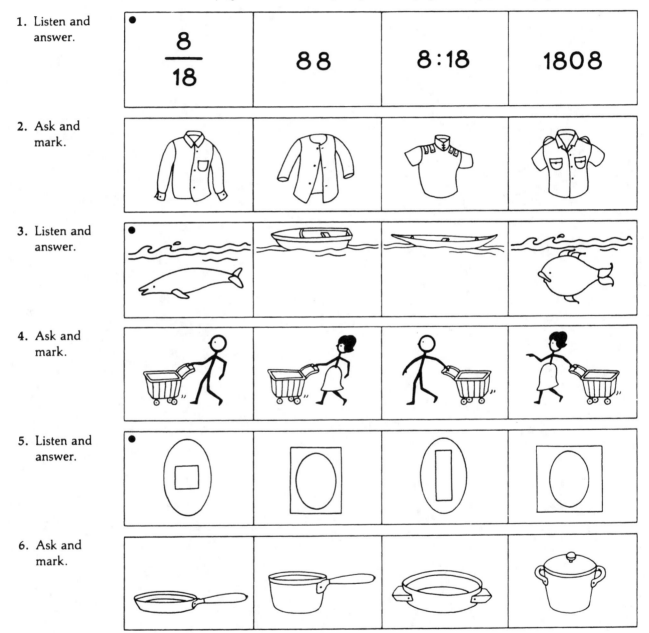

When you finish this exercise, show your page to your partner and compare your answers. Are they all the same? Which ones did you miss? If there is time, do the exercise again, but choose different pictures to ask questions about and make different marks on your page.

PART FOUR
CONSTRUCTING MEANINGFUL DIALOGS

To the Teacher

1. The exercises in Part Four require students to match sentences to create dialogs that "make sense." To be certain that students understand the meaning of the phrase "makes sense," give them an example. On the board, write a common question in English, such as:

   Q. "How are you today?"

   Then add a reply that does not make sense:

   A. "It's 2:30."

   Ask students to comment on the response. Is it okay? No? Why not? It doesn't make sense because it doesn't give the information requested.
   Try another example and ask students to explain their choices:

   Q. "Where are you going?"
   A.1. "Fine, thank you.
   A.2. "To the library."

   Encourage students to use the phrases "make(s) sense" and "does (or doesn't) make sense" in their explanations and in their subsequent performance of the activity.

2. Once students have understood the object of Part Four, you may want to introduce some of the following vocabulary and idioms used in the exercises. Since the purpose of the activity is to select appropriate sentences to construct meaningful dialogs, it is important that students be familiar with all or most of these words and expressions.

   Exercise 1
   A Bad Sore Throat: I wonder if; sore throat; fever; a hundred and two (degrees); headache, coughing; that's a good sign; it probably wouldn't hurt to . . .

   Dosages: druggist; vitamins; recommend; vitamin tablets; liquid; swallow; drops

   Remembering an Illness: pneumonia; strep throat; flu; didn't take care of myself; a temperature of . . .; expose yourself (to people with colds)

   Exercise 2
   Rainy Weather: What a day!; it looks like it's never going to stop; forecast; sure does; Boy! I don't see how you stand it; huh? nope

   Warm Weather: catch up with; sure is; me neither; 80 degrees (F); daydreaming; looking out the window; I'd rather be . . .

   Autumn Weather: the leaves are blowing in the wind; get tired of; I hope it lasts; it's going to be like this; eventually; winter will be here soon enough; in the meantime; give you some pointers

Exercise 3

A Legal Appointment: something's come up; do you have any idea when; squeeze me in

A Medical Appointment: receptionist; can't make my appointment; cancel; openings

An Appointment with a Colleague: handle it; kind of busy; some stuff; could you possibly . . . ?; inconvenient; it'll be about 45 minutes before I can get there

Exercise 4

A Problem with the Landlord: plumbing; clogged up; why didn't you come over?; borrow; leaking; light switches; plugs

A Problem with the Neighbors: dropped by; haven't slept in days; couldn't sleep a wink; shouting at each other; until all hours; flashlight; just as loud as ever; doesn't do a bit of good

A Problem with an Apartment: showing you around; counter space; it doesn't get particularly hot; I can't afford to . . .; thrift stores

Exercise 5

Shopping for Pans: frying pan; saucepan; start at; normally sells for . . .

Getting Advice About Shopping: how much . . . will (it) cost me?; that depends; I wouldn't get that kind; they keep breaking; that kind; much more than I can afford

Buying a Gift: you ought to be able to (get her something nice for . . .)

Exercise 6

A Big Hotel: lobby; go sightseeing; doorman; offers to get you a cab; you know . . .; everytime you turn around (somebody wants something); tip; at least that much; I'd rather . . .; wow!; travel agent; luggage; they figure (you mean a big one)

A Bad Hotel: in the first place; recommended; it faces the street

Another Hotel: new luxury hotels; a little side street; room service; it sounded like (the kind of place you'd like); lots of comfort

Exercise 7

Crime and Punishment: broken into; burglar; in jail for life; starving; punished; robbed; teach him a lesson; criminals; severely; committing crimes; preventing a crime; a simple problem

Theft: awful; stolen; lost; crowded

Cheating on an Exam: run into; be expelled; cheating on an exam; warned; that doesn't make it right

Exercise 8

At the University: English Composition; sorry to have bothered you; don't mention it

A Serious Discussion: reacted; obey; respect; even if . . . ?; what i.
. . . ?; besides; like what?

Wishing: park bench; gardeners; totally impractical; start from scratch

3. The completed dialogs appear in a separate section at the back of the book (pp. 101–108). Before you begin an exercise, you might want to make copies of the appropriate dialog "solutions" to hand out to students *after* they have finished the exercise.

4. Other dialog exercises of the same type, and further suggestions for their use, may be found in *Getting Along in English* by Adrian S. Palmer and Margot C. Kimball (New York: Longman, 1981).

Sample Exercise 4

The exercises in Part Four will give you practice in selecting sentences to form meaningful dialogs.

WHAT TO DO

You and your partner will each receive an exercise page. On each page there will be a description of three situations and numbered sentences forming three separate dialogs. You and your partner will take turns beginning a dialog. Then you will each select, mark, and read aloud sentences to build a dialog that makes sense. Look at example 1, below. The correct sentences are already marked (X).

1. TELEPHONE MESSAGES

If you are Partner A, begin with sentence 1:

Situation: It's 8 P.M. Your name is Pat. You are telephoning your friend Harry. Someone else answers the phone and says, "Hello."

1. Could I please speak with Harry? ✖

3. a. No, I don't mind waiting.
   b. Could you tell me when he'll be back? ✖

5. a. Yes. Will you tell him Pat called, please? ✖
   b. Yes. I'll send it right over.

If you are Partner B, begin with sentence 2:

Situation: It's 8 P.M. You live in a house with several people. The phone rings. You answer and say, "Hello."

2. a. I'm sorry, but he isn't here right now. ✖
   b. No, thank you, he doesn't.

4. a. Yes, she left here just a few minutes ago.
   b. He'll be back at 10:30. May I take a message? ✖

6. a. Sure, I'll be glad to. ✖
   b. Okay, you're welcome.

Now you try example 2. Listen carefully to your partner and make sure that your answers "make sense."

2. AT A BUS STOP

If you are Partner A, begin with sentence 1:

Situation: You are waiting at a bus stop and you want to go to the airport. You ask someone for information.

1. Excuse me, does this bus go to the airport?

3. a. Do you know when it arrives?
   b. Where does it go?

5. a. Oh no, I already missed it!
   b. Great! I'm just in time. Thanks.

If you are Partner B, begin with sentence 2:

Situation: You are waiting at a bus stop. A stranger asks you for information.

2. a. Yes, that one over there.
   b. No, you want the number 2 bus.

4. a. About two hours ago.
   b. In about 10 minutes.

6. a. That's okay.
   b. I'm sorry.

When you have finished an exercise, review your answers with your partner. Be sure to discuss your mistakes and any problems you had. Then, repeat the exercise with the same partner (exchange papers) or with a different partner, and use a different mark (✔).

(For the answers to example 2, see below.)

(Answers to Example 2: 1, 2b, 3a, 4b, 5b, 6a.)

Exercise 4.1

Instructions: You and your partner are going to have three short conversations. Read each situation and the sentences below it. Be sure you understand all the words. Then begin your dialog with sentence **1.** Listen carefully as your partner replies. Next select a response from **3, a** or **b,** and say it to your partner. After your partner replies again, select a response from **5, a** or **b.** When your partner replies the third time, the dialog is over. Do not look at your partner's page while you are doing this exercise. And remember to choose answers that make sense!

A BAD SORE THROAT

Situation: You have had a bad sore throat for three days. You wonder if you should call a doctor. You ask your partner for advice.

1. Have you ever had a bad sore throat?

3. **a.** You're lucky. I get three or four bad sore throats every winter.
   b. Well, my throat's been really sore for three days. I wonder if I should call the doctor.

5. **a.** No, I don't have a headache. But I've been coughing a lot.
   b. Yes. And I've been coughing a lot during the night.

DOSAGES

Situation: The doctor has told you to give your daughter vitamins. You are in the drugstore. Your partner is the druggist.

1. Excuse me, would you recommend these vitamin tablets for my little girl?

3. **a.** Oh, she's only three.
   b. Yes. The doctor told me she needed them.

5. **a.** I see. How many tablets should I give her?
   b. I see. How many drops should I give her?

REMEMBERING AN ILLNESS

Situation: You and your partner have been visiting a sick friend. On the way home, you begin to talk about illnesses you have had.

1. I'll never forget how sick I was when I had pneumonia.

3. **a.** Well, I was in the hospital for ten days.
   b. Oh, I had the flu and didn't take care of myself.

5. **a.** Well, I had a temperature of a hundred and four for three days.
   b. Sure. But I had to go to work every day.

When you finish this exercise, review your answers with your partner. Discuss your mistakes and any problems you had. If there is time, repeat the dialog with the same partner (exchange papers) or with a different partner.

Exercise 4.1

Instructions: You and your partner are going to have three short conversations. Read each situation and the sentences below it. Be sure you understand all the words. Listen carefully as your partner begins each dialog. Then select a response from **2, a** or **b,** and say it to your partner. After your partner replies, select a response from **4, a** or **b.** When your partner replies again, end the dialog with a sentence from **6, a** or **b.** Do not look at your partner's page while you are doing this exercise. And remember to choose answers that make sense!

A BAD SORE THROAT

Situation: Your partner does not look well.

2. **a.** Yes, several times. Why?

 b. A hundred and two! Have you seen a doctor?

4. **a.** Have you had a fever too?

 b. What did the doctor say?

6. **a.** Well, that's a good sign. You probably don't really need a doctor.

 b. Well, it probably wouldn't hurt to call the doctor.

DOSAGES

Situation: You are a druggist. Your partner is a customer, and asks your advice about some medicine.

2. **a.** How old is your daughter?

 b. How old is your son?

4. **a.** Well, I think the liquid would be better, then. It's easier for children to swallow.

 b. Well, I think the tablets would be better, then. They're a lot stronger.

6. **a.** I'd say two drops, three times a day. You can put it in her milk or juice if you want.

 b. Oh, not more than three or four days.

REMEMBERING AN ILLNESS

Situation: You and your partner have been visiting a sick friend. On the way home, you begin to talk about illnesses you have had.

2. **a.** Pneumonia! How did you get it?

 b. Strep throat! That's serious.

4. **a.** Yeah, you're right. You shouldn't expose yourself to people with colds.

 b. How sick were you?

6. **a.** A hundred and three! That's really high for an adult.

 b. A hundred and four! That's really high for an adult.

When you finish this exercise, review your answers with your partner. Discuss your mistakes and any problems you had. If there is time, repeat the dialog with the same partner (exchange papers) or with a different partner.

Exercise 4.2

PARTNER

Instructions: You and your partner are going to have three short conversations. Read each situation and the sentences below it. Be sure you understand all the words. Listen carefully as your partner begins each dialog. Then select a response from **2, a** or **b,** and say it to your partner. After your partner replies, select a response from **4, a** or **b.** When your partner replies again, end the dialog with a sentence from **6, a** or **b.** Do not look at your partner's page while you are doing this exercise. And remember to choose answers that make sense!

RAINY WEATHER

Situation: You are standing inside a store, waiting for it to stop raining so hard. Your partner comes into the store.

2. **a.** It looks like it'll never stop, doesn't it?

   b. Yeah. I've never seen so much rain. Does it rain like this all the time here?

4. **a.** I'm glad to hear that. It'd be awful if it went on day after day.

   b. Boy! I don't see how you stand it. We never have anything like this at home.

6. **a.** Nope. You get more rain in a week here than we get in a year at home.

   b. Yeah. And I forgot my umbrella, too.

WARM WEATHER

Situation: You are walking to school. Your partner catches up with you.

2. **a.** I don't know what you mean. This weather is beautiful!

   b. Yeah. Makes you want to be outside, doesn't it?

4. **a.** Oh, sitting under a tree with a good book.

   b. Me neither. I keep looking out the window and daydreaming.

6. **a.** Oh, I just think about all the things I'd rather be doing.

   b. Not me. I just get sleepy.

AUTUMN WEATHER

Situation: It is autumn, and the leaves are blowing in the wind. You are standing at a bus stop with your partner.

2. **a.** Not really. Windy weather makes me feel so good. I don't know why.

   b. Not really. I wish it were summer again.

4. **a.** Of course. I hope it lasts for weeks.

   b. Oh sure, eventually. But it won't be like this forever.

6. **a.** Winter will be here soon enough. In the meantime, I'm going to enjoy the fall!

   b. It's too bad you don't like skiing. I took a few lessons last winter, and I really enjoyed it.

When you finish this exercise, review your answers with your partner. Discuss your mistakes and any problems you had. If there is time, repeat the dialog with the same partner (exchange papers) or with a different partner.

Exercise 4.2

Instructions: You and your partner are going to have three short conversations. Read each situation and the sentences below it. Be sure you understand all the words. Then begin your dialog with sentence **1.** Listen carefully as your partner replies. Next select a response from **3, a** or **b,** and say it to your partner. After your partner replies again, select a response from **5, a** or **b.** When your partner replies the third time, the dialog is over. Do not look at your partner's page while you are doing this exercise. And remember to choose answers that make sense!

RAINY WEATHER

Situation: You walk into a store to get out of the rain, and you see your partner.

1. What a day! It looks like it's never going to stop raining.

3. **a.** No, the forecast this morning said we'll have at least three more days of it.

   b. Around this time of year it does. Sometimes you think it'll never stop.

5. **a.** Really? It doesn't rain much where you come from, huh?

   b. Really? It rained like this all the time there, huh?

WARM WEATHER

Situation: You are walking to school and catch up with your partner.

1. Sure is a great day, isn't it?

3. **a.** Yeah, really. I don't like going to class at all on a day like this.

   b. Oh, I'd say it's at least seventy five, maybe eighty degrees.

5. **a.** What do you think about?

   b. Well, I'd like to, but I really think I'd better go to class.

AUTUMN WEATHER

Situation: It is autumn, and the leaves are blowing in the wind. You are standing at a bus stop with your partner.

1. Don't you wish it were summer again?

3. **a.** You mean it's going to be like this all month? I'll get awfully tired of it.

   b. You mean you actually *like* this weather? Don't you get tired of it?

5. **a.** Well, I'm glad to hear that. If it can't be nice and warm, I'd rather have it snow, so I can go skiing.

   b. Well, why don't you do that? I know a lot about skiing and I could give you some pointers.

When you finish this exercise, review your answers with your partner. Discuss your mistakes and any problems you had. If there is time, repeat the dialog with the same partner (exchange papers) or with a different partner.

Exercise 4.3

(Exercise 4.3, A)

Instructions: You and your partner are going to have three short conversations. Read each situation and the sentences below it. Be sure you understand all the words. Then begin your dialog with sentence **1.** Listen carefully as your partner replies. Next select a response from **3, a** or **b,** and say it to your partner. After your partner replies again, select a response from **5, a** or **b.** When your partner replies the third time, the dialog is over. Do not look at your partner's page while you are doing this exercise. And remember to choose answers that make sense!

A LEGAL APPOINTMENT

Situation: You are calling your lawyer, Ms. Bell. Her secretary (your partner) has just answered the phone, saying, "Good morning. Law office."

1. Hello. This is _____your full name_____. Something's come up, and I've got to see Ms. Bell right away.

3. a. Well, do you have any idea where she's gone?
   b. Well, when do you think the meeting will be over?

5. a. Look, it's very important for me to see Ms. Bell this morning. Couldn't you squeeze me in for fifteen minutes at ten o'clock?
   b. Well, it's extremely important for me to see Ms. Bell this morning. Could you call me back when you find out how long the meeting will be?

A MEDICAL APPOINTMENT

Situation: You are calling your doctor. His receptionist (your partner) has just said, "Good afternoon. Dr. Spear's office."

1. Hello. This is _____your full name_____. I'm afraid I can't make my appointment tomorrow.

3. a. Yes. It was for ten—tomorrow at ten.
   b. Yes. Do you have any openings next week?

5. a. Well, do you have one in the late afternoon the day after tomorrow?
   b. Well, that's okay. I can wait until then, but I'd like it as early in the day as possible.

AN APPOINTMENT WITH A COLLEAGUE

Situation: You and your partner work together in an office downtown. It is Saturday morning, and you are at home. You have just finished talking to your boss about some important work she needs you to do today. You have to discuss it with your partner, so you call your partner at home. He or she has just said, "Hello."

1. Hello, _____partner's first name_____. This is _____your first name_____. Could I meet you sometime this morning? I need to talk to you about something important.

3. a. Sorry. I need to show you some stuff. Can't we get together sometime this morning?
   b. Yeah, that's a good idea. Can you be here by eleven o'clock?

5. a. No, I have to stay here. I'm waiting for the boss to call me back. Could you possibly come to my place?
   b. No, that's too inconvenient for you. Why don't we meet at your place?

When you finish this exercise, review your answers with your partner. Discuss your mistakes and any problems you had. If there is time, repeat the dialog with the same partner (exchange papers) or with a different partner.

Exercise 4.3

Instructions: You and your partner are going to have three short conversations. Read each situation and the sentences below it. Be sure you understand all the words. Listen carefully as your partner begins each dialog. Then select a response from **2, a** or **b**, and say it to your partner. After your partner replies, select a response from **4, a** or **b**. When your partner replies again, end the dialog with a sentence from **6, a** or **b**. Do not look at your partner's page while you are doing this exercise. And remember to choose answers that make sense!

A LEGAL APPOINTMENT

Situation: You are the secretary for several lawyers, including Ms. Bell. The phone has just rung, and you have answered it, saying, "Good morning. Law office."

2. a. I'm sorry, Mr./Mrs./Ms. ___partner's last name___, but Ms. Bell is in a meeting.

   b. I'm sorry, Mr./Mrs./Ms. ___partner's last name___, but Ms. Bell won't be in at all tomorrow. How about the next day?

4. a. Oh, it should be over by ten o'clock, I think. But Ms. Bell has to be at the airport by 10:45.

   b. No, I'm sorry, she already has an appointment for that time. I could give you one half an hour earlier, though.

6. a. Well, all right, Mr./Mrs./Ms. ___your partner's last name___. But only for 15 minutes.

   b. All right, Mr./Mrs./Ms. ___your partner's last name___, I'll have her call you right at eleven.

A MEDICAL APPOINTMENT

Situation: You are a doctor's receptionist. The phone has just rung, and you have answered it, saying "Good afternoon. Dr. Spear's office."

2. a. Yes, Mr./Mrs./Ms. ___partner's last name___, it's tomorrow at ten.

   b. All right, Mr./Mrs./Ms. ___partner's last name___, I'll cancel it for you. Would you like to make another one now?

4. a. No, I'm sorry. The doctor will be out of town all next week. The first opening I have is a week from Monday.

   b. No, I'm sorry. The doctor will be out of town that day. How about the day after that?

6. a. Okay. I'll put you down for 8:30 Monday morning, then.

   b. Okay. I'll put you down for 4:00 that day, then.

AN APPOINTMENT WITH A COLLEAGUE

Situation: You and your partner work together in an office downtown. It is Saturday morning, and you are at home. The phone has just rung, and you have answered it, saying, "Hello."

2. a. Well, couldn't we handle it on the phone now? I'll be kind of busy this morning.

   b. Sorry, I'm not free this afternoon.

4. a. Fine. I'll call you back this evening, when I get home.

   b. Well, okay. Why don't you come over here to my house?

6. a. Oh well, I guess so. But it'll be about 45 minutes before I can get there.

   b. Okay. I'll wait for you here. We can have lunch while we talk.

When you finish this exercise, review your answers with your partner. Discuss your mistakes and any problems you had. If there is time, repeat the dialog with the same partner (exchange papers) or with a different partner.

Exercise 4.4

Instructions: You and your partner are going to have three short conversations. Read each situation and the sentences below it. Be sure you understand all the words. Listen carefully as your partner begins each dialog. Then select a response from **2, a** or **b,** and say it to your partner. After your partner replies, select a response from **4, a** or **b.** When your partner replies again, end the dialog with a sentence from **6, a** or **b.** Do not look at your partner's page while you are doing this exercise. And remember to choose answers that make sense!

A PROBLEM WITH THE LANDLORD

Situation: Your partner is late for a meeting with you.

2. **a.** Oh, no! Is your plumbing clogged up again?
   b. Oh, no! Why didn't you come over and borrow one from me?

4. **a.** Oh? Where was it leaking?
   b. Oh? What's the problem?

6. **a.** I know what you mean. Had you told him about the problem before?
   b. I know what you mean. I usually have to call my landlord five or six times before I can get anything fixed.

A PROBLEM WITH THE NEIGHBORS

Situation: Your partner has just dropped by for a visit.

2. **a.** Oh, it was the old couple next door. I've just been getting their sink unclogged for them.
   b. Oh, it's my upstairs neighbors. I couldn't sleep a wink last night.

4. **a.** Not this time. *This* time they were shouting at each other all night long.
   b. Not this time. *This* time they had a noisy party until all hours.

6. **a.** Oh, I've tried that before. But after the police leave, they're just as loud as ever.
   b. Oh, I've tried that before. But it doesn't do a bit of good.

A PROBLEM WITH AN APARTMENT

Situation: You have been showing your partner around your new apartment.

2. **a.** What's the matter? Is your living room too small?
   b. What's the matter? Is your kitchen too small?

4. **a.** Well, why don't you get the stove fixed, then?
   b. Well, why don't you put in a table, then?

6. **a.** You wouldn't have to buy a new one. Check the prices for used furniture at the thrift stores.
   b. Well, I don't know. Mine's gas, and I like it all right.

When you finish this exercise, review your answers with your partner. Discuss your mistakes and any problems you had. If there is time, repeat the dialog with the same partner (exchange papers) or with a different partner.

Exercise 4.4

Instructions: You and your partner are going to have three short conversations. Read each situation and the sentences below it. Be sure you understand all the words. Then begin your dialog with sentence **1**. Listen carefully as your partner replies. Next select a response from **3, a** or **b**, and say it to your partner. After your partner replies again, select a response from **5, a** or **b.** When your partner replies the third time, the dialog is over. Do not look at your partner's page while you are doing this exercise. And remember to choose answers that make sense!

A PROBLEM WITH THE LANDLORD

Situation: You are late for a meeting with your partner.

1. Sorry I'm late. I've spent the last half hour talking to my landlord.

3. **a.** No, not this time. Now it's the plumbing.

   b. No, not this time. Now it's the electricity.

5. **a.** Oh, two light switches and some of the plugs haven't been working. I'd called the landlord about them three times already, but he *still* hadn't fixed anything.

   b. Yeah, this morning. Just as I turned on the stove, all the electricity in the apartment went off.

A PROBLEM WITH THE NEIGHBORS

Situation: You have dropped by to visit your partner.

1. You look like you haven't slept in days! What's the matter?

3. **a.** Why? Did they have another noisy party?

   b. Why? Couldn't you find a flashlight?

5. **a.** Why didn't you go up and complain, then?

   b. How long did their party last?

A PROBLEM WITH AN APARTMENT

Situation: Your partner has been showing you around her or his new apartment.

1. I really hate the kitchen in my apartment. I don't even like to cook anymore.

3. **a.** No, it's big enough—more than enough room. But there's not enough counter space to work on.

   b. No, it doesn't get particularly hot, but I wish it had a window.

5. **a.** Well, I would, but I don't know how to.

   b. Oh, I can't afford to buy one. And the landlady certainly won't buy one for me.

When you finish this exercise, review your answers with your partner. Discuss your mistakes and any problems you had. If there is time, repeat the dialog with the same partner (exchange papers) or with a different partner.

Exercise 4.5

Instructions: You and your partner are going to have three short conversations. Read each situation and the sentences below it. Be sure you understand all the words. Then begin your dialog with sentence **1.** Listen carefully as your partner replies. Next select a response from **3, a** or **b,** and say it to your partner. After your partner replies again, select a response from **5, a** or **b.** When your partner replies the third time, the dialog is over. Do not look at your partner's page while you are doing this exercise. And remember to choose answers that make sense!

SHOPPING FOR PANS

Situation: You are shopping for a frying pan. Your partner is a salesclerk.

1. I'm looking for a frying pan.

3. **a.** Hmm. Do you have something a little less expensive?
   b. Well, do you have anything under twenty dollars?

5. **a.** No, that's still too expensive. Do you have one for around ten dollars?
   b. No, that one's too small. What else do you have?

GETTING ADVICE ABOUT SHOPPING

Situation: You want to buy a tape recorder, but you need help. You ask your partner for advice.

1. How much to you think a tape recorder will cost me?

3. **a.** I want it mostly for learning English, but I'd like to listen to music too.
   b. Eighty dollars! Oh, that's much more than I can afford.

5. **a.** Are you sure a cheap one will be good enough?
   b. And how much does "a pretty good one" cost?

BUYING A GIFT

Situation: You need to buy a gift for your aunt, but you don't know what to get her. You ask a partner for advice.

1. Do you have any ideas about what I could get my aunt for her birthday?

3. **a.** Oh, not more than ten dollars.
   b. Oh, she already has a lot of beautiful jewelry.

5. **a.** No. She never wears perfume. Maybe some flowers.
   b. No. She doesn't like to read. I thought I might get her some candy.

When you finish this exercise, review your answers with your partner. Discuss your mistakes and any problems you had. If there is time, repeat the dialog with the same partner (exchange papers) or with a different partner.

Exercise 4.5

Instructions: You and your partner are going to have three short conversations. Read each situation and the sentences below it. Be sure you understand all the words. Listen carefully as your partner begins each dialog. Then select a response from **2, a** or **b,** and say it to your partner. After your partner replies, select a response from **4, a** or **b.** When your partner replies again, end the dialog with a sentence from **6, a** or **b.** Do not look at your partner's page while you are doing this exercise. And remember to choose answers that make sense!

SHOPPING FOR PANS

Situation: You are a salesclerk in a store. Your partner is a customer.

2. **a.** Yes, ma'am/sir. Our saucepans start at $11.98.
   b. Well, this is a nice one. It's $15.95.

4. **a.** Yes. Here's one that's less. It sells for $8.50.
   b. Of course. Here's an electric one that sells for $24.89.

6. **a.** Well, here's a bigger one. It normally sells for $10.95, but it's on sale for half price today.
   b. Well, here's a smaller one. It normally sells for $8.95, but it's on sale for half price today.

GETTING ADVICE ABOUT SHOPPING

Situation: Your partner wants to buy a tape recorder and needs some help. She or he asks you for advice.

2. **a.** Well, that depends. Do you want to play music on it or just practice your pronunciation?
   b. Well, I wouldn't get that kind. They keep breaking.

4. **a.** Well, if you're only using it to learn English, you don't need a very expensive one.
   b. All right. Then you should get a pretty good one.

6. **a.** Oh, between forty and fifty dollars.
   b. Yes, that kind would be perfect for you.

BUYING A GIFT

Situation: Your partner needs to buy a gift for someone and asks you for advice.

2. **a.** Well, what does your mother want to do?
   b. Well, how much do you want to spend?

4. **a.** Hmm, let's see now. What about perfume?
   b. Hmm, let's see now. You ought to be able to get her a nice scarf for fifteen dollars.

6. **a.** That's a good idea. Most people like flowers.
   b. That's a good idea. Most people like candy.

When you finish this exercise, review your answers with your partner. Discuss your mistakes and any problems you had. If there is time, repeat the dialog with the same partner (exchange papers) or with a different partner.

Exercise 4.6

PARTNER

Instructions: You and your partner are going to have three short conversations. Read each situation and the sentences below it. Be sure you understand all the words. Then begin your dialog with sentence **1.** Listen carefully as your partner replies. Next select a response from **3, a** or **b,** and say it to your partner. After your partner replies again, select a response from **5, a** or **b.** When your partner replies the third time, the dialog is over. Do not look at your partner's page while you are doing this exercise. And remember to choose answers that make sense!

Your partner is a tourist visiting the city where you live and staying in a hotel.

A BIG HOTEL

Situation: You have met your partner in the lobby of your partner's hotel. As you leave to go sightseeing, the doorman opens the door for you and offers to get you a cab, but you and your partner prefer to walk. Now you are talking about what just happened.

2. a. You don't like that, huh?
   b. Who was the call from?

4. a. Wow! I'd never pay *that* much for a room.
   b. So would I. That's why I always pick a small, inexpensive hotel when I travel.

6. a. I agree. It *is* nice to have help with your luggage, and I usually have a lot of it.
   b. Yeah. If you just say "a good hotel," they figure you mean a big one.

A BAD HOTEL

Situation: You have met your partner in the lobby of your partner's hotel. You are going out together, and now you're talking about the hotel.

2. a. No, it's not very expensive, but the food is the best I've ever had.
   b. Why? What's wrong with it?

4. a. Uh-oh. That *is* bad.
   b. How do you know?

6. a. You ought to move into a different hotel.
   b. Why didn't you shut the window?

ANOTHER HOTEL

Situation: You meet your partner in a restaurant, where your **partner is now** telling you about a new hotel.

2. a. Is there something the matter with it?
   b. Are you staying at one of the new luxury hotels they've built downtown?

4. a. Well, what do you like about it, then?
   b. Boy, I wouldn't pay those prices!

6. a. Not me. I can't sleep if there's any noise.
   b. Not me. When I'm on vacation I like lots of comfort.

Exercise 4.6

(Exercise 4.6, B)

You are a tourist visiting a city where your partner lives. You are staying in a hotel.

A BIG HOTEL

Situation: Your partner has met you in the lobby of your hotel. As you leave to go sightseeing, the doorman opens the door for you and offers to get you a cab, but you and your partner prefer to walk. Now you are talking about what just happened.

1. You know, every time you turn around in that place, somebody wants to do something for you. And usually you have to tip them.

3. a. Oh, at least that much—maybe more.

   b. No, I wish they'd leave me alone. I'd rather do things for myself.

5. a. What kind of hotel do you like when you travel?

   b. I should have told my travel agent more about what I wanted, I guess.

A BAD HOTEL

Situation: Your partner has met you in the lobby of your hotel. You are going out together, and now you're talking about the hotel.

1. I'll never stay at *this* hotel again!

3. a. Well, in the first place, there's so much noise I couldn't sleep last night.

   b. Because my parents always used to stay here, and they recommended it.

5. a. And besides, I had to open the window, because the air conditioning wouldn't work.

   b. On the fifteenth floor. But it faces the street.

ANOTHER HOTEL

Situation: You have just spent one night in a little hotel you've discovered. You meet your partner in a restaurant, where you're now telling your partner about the new hotel.

1. You know, I really like my hotel. It's just what I need.

3. a. Oh, it's on a little side street not far from here.

   b. No, it's just a plain little hotel. It doesn't even have room service.

5. a. Yeah, I thought it sounded like the kind of place you'd like.

   b. Well, for one thing, the room is clean. And it's quiet. Those are the things I care about.

Instructions: You and your partner are going to have three short conversations. Read each situation and the sentences below it. Be sure you understand all the words. Listen carefully as your partner begins each dialog. Then select a response from **2, a** or **b,** and say it to your partner. After your partner replies, select a response from **4, a** or **b.** When your partner replies again, end the dialog with a sentence from **6, a** or **b.** Do not look at your partner's page while you are doing this exercise. And remember to choose answers that make sense!

When you finish this exercise, review your answers with your partner. Discuss your mistakes and any problems you had. If there is time, repeat the dialog with the same partner (exchange papers) or with a different partner.

Exercise 4.7

Instructions: You and your partner are going to have three short conversations. Read each situation and the sentences below it. Be sure you understand all the words. Then begin your dialog with sentence **1.** Listen carefully as your partner replies. Next select a response from **3, a** or **b,** and say it to your partner. After your partner replies again, select a response from **5, a** or **b.** When your partner replies the third time, the dialog is over. Do not look at your partner's page while you are doing this exercise. And remember to choose answers that make sense!

CRIME AND PUNISHMENT

Situation: Your partner's house was broken into last week. The police caught the burglar and returned what was stolen. Now, you and your partner are discussing how the burglar should be punished.

1. They ought to put that burglar in jail for life.

3. **a.** Do you know why he robbed you?
   b. How do you think he should be punished, then?

5. **a.** But if they don't punish criminals severely, what will prevent people from committing crimes?
   b. Do you really think two days in jail would teach him a lesson?

THEFT

Situation: One of your friends was just robbed. You are telling your partner what happened.

1. An awful thing happened to Randy. His wallet was stolen.

3. **a.** Ten dollars. But he lost all of his I.D. and credit cards too.
   b. In his room. The door was locked too.

5. **a.** They found it already? That's really fast work!
   b. Oh, he was on a crowded bus, and when he got off his wallet was gone.

CHEATING ON AN EXAM

Situation: You have just heard that several students were expelled from school. You run into your partner in the cafeteria, and start telling your partner the news.

1. Did you hear that five students were expelled for cheating on the exam?

3. **a.** Well, cheating is serious. I think they should be expelled.
   b. Making them pay a fine wouldn't help. They'd just cheat again.

5. **a.** But that doesn't make it right.
   b. Yeah, it's lucky only a few people cheat.

When you finish this exercise, review your answers with your partner. Discuss your mistakes and any problems you had. If there is time, repeat the dialog with the same partner (exchange papers) or with a different partner.

Exercise 4.7

Instructions: You and your partner are going to have three short conversations. Read each situation and the sentences below it. Be sure you understand all the words. Listen carefully as your partner begins each dialog. Then select a response from **2, a** or **b,** and say it to your partner. After your partner replies, select a response from **4, a** or **b.** When your partner replies again, end the dialog with a sentence from **6, a** or **b.** Do not look at your partner's page while you are doing this exercise. And remember to choose answers that make sense!

CRIME AND PUNISHMENT

Situation: Your house was broken into last week. The police caught the burglar and returned what was stolen. Now, you and your partner are discussing how the burglar should be punished.

2. **a.** Well, he isn't a bad man. It's just that his family was starving.
   b. How do you think he should be punished?

4. **a.** But after all, we did get back everything he'd stolen.
   b. Oh, maybe they should just put him in jail for a week or two to teach him a lesson.

6. **a.** I don't know. But preventing crime isn't a simple problem.
   b. You're right. Punishment probably doesn't work.

THEFT

Situation: Your partner tells you something that happened to your friend Randy.

2. **a.** No! Did he leave the key in the car?
   b. No! How much was in it?

4. **a.** How did it happen?
   b. A hundred dollars! Why was he carrying so much money?

6. **a.** Well, he shouldn't have left his door unlocked.
   b. Well, the police will never find it.

CHEATING ON AN EXAM

Situation: You run into your partner in the school cafeteria. He or she has some interesting news.

2. **a.** Expelled! Oh, that's too hard. They should have just been warned not to cheat again.
   b. That's awful! How many were expelled?

4. **a.** I agree. Cheating isn't really serious. Everyone does it.
   b. Not me. Everyone cheats once in a while.

6. **a.** I agree. Sometimes it's all right to cheat.
   b. Oh, I guess not. But I still think they shouldn't be expelled.

When you finish this exercise, review your answers with your partner. Discuss your mistakes and any problems you had. If there is time, repeat the dialog with the same partner (exchange papers) or with a different partner.

Exercise 4.8

Instructions: You and your partner are going to have three short conversations. Read each situation and the sentences below it. Be sure you understand all the words. Listen carefully as your partner begins each dialog. Then select a response from **2, a** or **b,** and say it to your partner. After your partner replies, select a response from **4, a** or **b.** When your partner replies again, end the dialog with a sentence from **6, a** or **b.** Do not look at your partner's page while you are doing this exercise. And remember to choose answers that make sense!

AT THE UNIVERSITY

Situation: You are a teacher at a university. You are on the second floor, walking to your office, when you pass a lost-looking student (your partner) who asks you for directions.

2. **a.** Dr. Jean English, or Dr. Michael English? They have offices on different floors.

   b. Do you want English Literature or English Composition? They're on different floors.

4. **a.** Well, if you don't know which, maybe Mrs. Johnson can help you. Her office is right there, through the door marked "Secretary."

   b. I see. Well, just go straight down this hall—it's the last office on the right.

6. **a.** No, I don't think so. But you could ask.

   b. Oh, that's okay. Don't mention it.

A SERIOUS DISCUSSION

Situation: You and your partner have been talking about the trouble your friend Pat got into, and how Pat's parents reacted. Then the conversation gets more serious.

2. **a.** Of course—at least, while they're living with them they should.

   b. What do you mean by "respect"?

4. **a.** Like what?

   b. Like who?

6. **a.** But how can you know if you'll be happy or not? Besides, parents have a lot more experience than their children do.

   b. Well, you don't really know if you'll like the job or not. And it's important to take care of your parents.

WISHING

Situation: You and your partner have been sitting together on a park bench, sometimes talking and sometimes not, as you watch the people go by.

2. **a.** Oh, I'd have a really beautiful house with a big garden around it, and a couple of gardeners to take care of it.

   b. That sounds fantastic. But, I mean—it's totally impractical, isn't it?

4. **a.** Well, I'd rather buy one. It takes too long if you start from scratch.

   b. In the city, of course—in a rich neighborhood.

6. **a.** So would I. I'd hate living in the country.

   b. You would? But in the city you're close to stores and movies and things.

When you finish this exercise, review your answers with your partner. Discuss your mistakes and any problems you had. If there is time, repeat the dialog with the same partner (exchange papers) or with a different partner.

Exercise 4.8

Instructions: You and your partner are going to have three short conversations. Read each situation and the sentences below it. Be sure you understand all the words. Then begin your dialog with sentence **1.** Listen carefully as your partner replies. Next select a response from **3, a** or **b,** and say it to your partner. After your partner replies again, select a response from **5, a** or **b.** When your partner replies the third time, the dialog is over. Do not look at your partner's page while you are doing this exercise. And remember to choose answers that make sense!

AT THE UNIVERSITY

Situation: You have found the building you want on a university campus, but you can't seem to find the right office. You stop a friendly-looking teacher (your partner) in the hall.

1. Excuse me. I'm looking for the English Department.

3. **a.** You mean those stairs over there?

   b. Oh. English Composition. I need some information about English 100.

5. **a.** Thanks. I'm sorry to have bothered you.

   b. I'm sorry. After I turn right at the end of the hall, did you say I go up the stairs, or down the stairs?

A SERIOUS DISCUSSION

Situation: You and your partner have been talking about the trouble your friend Pat got into, and how Pat's parents reacted. Then the conversation gets more serious.

1. Do you think children should obey their parents?

3. **a.** Even if they want their children to do something that's bad for them?

   b. Well, maybe not. But what if they *are* still living with their parents?

5. **a.** That's stupid! Of course parents should love their children.

   b. Like marrying someone they won't be happy with.

WISHING

Situation: You and your partner have been sitting together on a park bench, sometimes talking and sometimes not, as you watch the people go by.

1. If you were rich, what kind of house would you want?

3. **a.** Not me. I'd want a house with a big garden.

   b. In the city or in the country?

5. **a.** Really? I'd hate living in the country.

   b. Really? I'd hate living in the city.

When you finish this exercise, review your answers with your partner. Discuss your mistakes and any problems you had. If there is time, repeat the dialog with the same partner (exchange papers) or with a different partner.

Dialog Solutions

Dialog Solution 4.1

A BAD SORE THROAT

1. Have you ever had a bad sore throat?

2. Yes, several times. Why?

3. Well, my throat's been really sore for three days. I wonder if I should call the doctor.

4. Have you had a fever too?

5. Yes. And I've been coughing a lot during the night.

6. Well, it probably wouldn't hurt to call the doctor.

DOSAGES

1. Excuse me, would you recommend these vitamin tablets for my little girl?

2. How old is your daughter?

3. Oh, she's only three.

4. Well, I think the liquid would be better, then. It's easier for children to swallow.

5. I see. How many drops should I give her?

6. I'd say two drops, three times a day. You can put it in her milk or juice if you want.

REMEMBERING AN ILLNESS

1. I'll never forget how sick I was when I had pneumonia.

2. Pneumonia! How did you get it?

3. Oh, I had the flu and didn't take care of myself.

4. How sick were you?

5. Well, I had a temperature of a hundred and four for three days.

6. A hundred and four! That's really high for an adult.

Dialog Solution 4.2

RAINY WEATHER

1. What a day! It looks like it's never going to stop raining.
2. Yeah. I've never seen so much rain. Does it rain like this all the time here?
3. Around this time of year it does. Sometimes you think it'll never stop.
4. Boy! I don't see how you stand it. We never have anything like this at home.
5. Really? It doesn't rain much where you come from, huh?
6. Nope. You get more rain in a week here than we get in a year at home.

WARM WEATHER

1. Sure is a great day, isn't it?
2. Yeah. Makes you want to be outside, doesn't it?
3. Yeah, really. I don't like going to class at all on a day like this.
4. Me neither. I keep looking out the window and daydreaming.
5. What do you think about?
6. Oh, I just think about all the things I'd rather be doing.

AUTUMN WEATHER

1. Don't you wish it were summer again?
2. Not really. Windy weather makes me feel so good. I don't know why.
3. You mean you actually *like* this weather? Don't you get tired of it?
4. Oh sure, eventually. But it won't be like this forever.
5. Well, I'm glad to hear that. If it can't be nice and warm, I'd rather have it snow, so I can go skiing.
6. Winter will be here soon enough. In the meantime, I'm going to enjoy the fall!

Dialog Solution 4.3

A LEGAL APPOINTMENT

1. Hello. This is _____your full name_____. Something's come up, and I've got to see Ms. Bell right away.
2. I'm sorry, Mr./Mrs./Ms. _____partner's last name_____, but Ms. Bell is in a meeting.
3. Well, when do you think the meeting will be over?
4. Oh, it should be over by ten o'clock, I think. But Ms. Bell has to be at the airport by 10:45.
5. Look, it's very important for me to see Ms. Bell this morning. Couldn't you squeeze me in for fifteen minutes at ten o'clock?
6. Well, all right, Mr./Mrs./Ms. _____partner's last name_____. But only for 15 minutes.

A MEDICAL APPOINTMENT

1. Hello. This is _____your full name_____. I'm afraid I can't make my appointment tomorrow.
2. All right, Mr./Mrs./Ms. _____partner's last name_____, I'll cancel it for you. Would you like to make another one now?
3. Yes. Do you have any openings next week?
4. No, I'm sorry. The doctor will be out of town all next week. The first opening I have is a week from Monday.
5. Well, that's okay. I can wait until then. But I'd like it as early in the day as possible.
6. Okay. I'll put you down for 8:30 Monday morning, then.

AN APPOINTMENT WITH A COLLEAGUE

1. Hello, _____partner's first name_____. This is _____your first name_____. Could I meet you sometime this morning? I need to talk to you about something important.
2. Well, couldn't we handle it on the phone now? I'll be kind of busy this morning.
3. Sorry. I need to show you some stuff. Can't we get together sometime this morning?
4. Well, okay. Why don't you come over here to my house?
5. No, I have to stay here. I'm waiting for the boss to call me back. Could you possibly come to my place?
6. Oh well, I guess so. But it'll be about 45 minutes before I can get there.

Dialog Solution 4.4

A PROBLEM WITH THE LANDLORD

1. Sorry I'm late. I've spent the last half hour talking to my landlord.
2. Oh, no! Is your plumbing clogged up again?
3. No, not this time. Now it's the electricity.
4. Oh? What's the problem?
5. Oh, two light switches and some of the plugs haven't been working. I'd called the landlord about them three times already, but he *still* hadn't fixed anything.
6. I know what you mean. I usually have to call my landlord five or six times before I can get anything fixed.

A PROBLEM WITH THE NEIGHBORS

1. You look like you haven't slept in days! What's the matter?
2. Oh, it's my upstairs neighbors. I couldn't sleep a wink last night.
3. Why? Did they have another noisy party?
4. Not this time. *This* time they were shouting at each other all night long.
5. Why didn't you go up and complain, then?
6. Oh, I've tried that before. But it doesn't do a bit of good.

A PROBLEM WITH AN APARTMENT

1. I really hate the kitchen in my apartment. I don't even like to cook anymore.
2. What's the matter? Is your kitchen too small?
3. No, it's big enough—more than enough room. But there's not enough counter space to work on.
4. Well, why don't you put in a table, then?
5. Oh, I can't afford to buy one. And the landlady certainly won't buy one for me.
6. You wouldn't have to buy a new one. Check the prices for used furniture at the thrift stores.

Dialog Solution 4.5

SHOPPING FOR PANS

1. I'm looking for a frying pan.
2. Well, this is a nice one. It's $15.95.
3. Hmm. Do you have something a little less expensive?
4. Yes. Here's one that's less. It sells for $8.50.
5. No, that one's too small. What else do you have?
6. Well, here's a bigger one. It normally sells for $10.95, but it's on sale for half price today.

GETTING ADVICE ABOUT SHOPPING

1. How much do you think a tape recorder will cost me?
2. Well, that depends. Do you want to play music on it or just practice your pronunciation?
3. I want it mostly for learning English, but I'd like to listen to music too.
4. All right. Then you should get a pretty good one.
5. And how much does "a pretty good one" cost?
6. Oh, between forty and fifty dollars.

BUYING A GIFT

1. Do you have any ideas about what I could get my aunt for her birthday?
2. Well, how much do you want to spend?
3. Oh, not more than ten dollars.
4. Hmm, let's see now. What about perfume?
5. No. She never wears perfume. Maybe some flowers.
6. That's a good idea. Most people like flowers.

Dialog Solution 4.6

A BIG HOTEL

1. You know, every time you turn around in that place, somebody wants to do something for you. And usually you have to tip them.
2. You don't like that, huh?
3. No, I wish they'd leave me alone. I'd rather do things for myself.
4. So would I. That's why I always pick a small, inexpensive hotel when I travel.
5. I should have told my travel agent more about what I wanted, I guess.
6. Yeah. If you just say "a good hotel," they figure you mean a big one.

A BAD HOTEL

1. I'll never stay at *this* hotel again!
2. Why? What's wrong with it?
3. Well, in the first place, there's so much noise I couldn't sleep last night.
4. Uh-oh. That *is* bad.
5. And besides, I had to open the window because the air conditioning wouldn't work.
6. You ought to move into a different hotel.

ANOTHER HOTEL

1. You know, I really like my hotel. It's just what I need.
2. Are you staying at one of the new luxury hotels they've built downtown?
3. No, it's just a plain little hotel. It doesn't even have room service.
4. Well, what do you like about it, then?
5. Well, for one thing, the room is clean. And it's quiet. Those are the things I care about.
6. Not me. When I'm on vacation I like lots of comfort.

Dialog Solution 4.7

CRIME AND PUNISHMENT

1. They ought to put that burglar in jail for life.
2. Well, he isn't a bad man. It's just that his family was starving.
3. How do you think he should be punished, then?
4. Oh, maybe they should just put him in jail for a week or two to teach him a lesson.
5. But if they don't punish criminals severely, what will prevent people from committing crimes?
6. I don't know. But preventing crime isn't a simple problem.

THEFT

1. An awful thing happened to Randy. His wallet was stolen.
2. No! how much was in it?
3. Ten dollars. But he lost all of his I.D. and credit cards too.
4. How did it happen?
5. Oh, he was on a crowded bus, and when he got off his wallet was gone.
6. Well, the police will never find it.

CHEATING ON AN EXAM

1. Did you hear that five students were expelled for cheating on the exam?
2. Expelled! Oh, that's too hard. They should have just been warned not to cheat again.
3. Well, cheating is serious. I think they should be expelled.
4. Not me. Everyone cheats once in a while.
5. But that doesn't make it right.
6. Oh, I guess not. But I still think they shouldn't be expelled.

Dialog Solution 4.8

AT THE UNIVERSITY

1. Excuse me. I'm looking for the English Department.
2. Do you want English Literature or English Composition? They're on different floors.
3. Oh. English Composition. I need some information about English 100.
4. I see. Well, just go straight down this hall—it's the last office on the right.
5. Thanks. I'm sorry to have bothered you.
6. Oh, that's okay. Don't mention it.

A SERIOUS DISCUSSION

1. Do you think children should obey their parents?
2. Of course—at least, while they're living with them they should.
3. Even if they want their children to do something that's bad for them?
4. Like what?
5. Like marrying someone they won't be happy with.
6. But how can you know if you'll be happy or not? Besides, parents have a lot more experience than their children do.

WISHING

1. If you were rich, what kind of house would you want?
2. Oh, I'd have a really beautiful house with a big garden around it, and a couple of gardeners to take care of it.
3. In the city or in the country?
4. In the city, of course—in a rich neighborhood.
5. Really? I'd hate living in the city.
6. You would? But in the city you're close to stores and movies and things.